Issues in Education

GENERAL EDITOR: PHILIP HILLS

Education in a Multicultural Society

Other books in this series

Gordon Batho: Political Issues in Education
David Bosworth: Open Learning
Paul Fisher: Education 2000
Michael Williams: In-Service Education and Training

Roy Todd

Education in a Multicultural Society

CASSELL

Cassell Educational Limited
Villiers House
41/47 Strand
London WC2N 5JE

First published 1991

British Library Cataloguing in Publication Data
Todd, Roy
    Education in a multicultural society.—(Issues in
    Education)
    1. Great Britain. Education. Implications
    I. Title   II. Series
    370.19342

ISBN   0-304-32301-2 (hardback)
        0-304-31952-X (paperback)

Phototypeset by Input Typesetting Ltd.,
London SW19 8DR
Printed and bound in Great Britain by
Biddles Ltd, Guildford and King's Lynn

Contents

Foreword: The purpose of this series

The educational scene is changing rapidly. This change is being caused by a complexity of factors which includes a re-examination of present educational provision against a background of changing social and economic policies, the 1988 Education Reform Act, new forms of testing and assessment, a National Curriculum, and local management of schools with more participation by parents.

As the educational process is concerned with every aspect of our lives and our society both now and for the future, it is of vital importance that all teachers, teachers in training, administrators and educational policy-makers should be aware and informed on current issues in education.

This series of books is thus designed to inform on current issues, look at emerging ones, and to give an authoritative overview which will be of immense help to all those involved in the education process.

Philip Hills
Cambridge

Preface

The transformation of British society by the migration of people from the 'New Commonwealth' and Pakistan in the 1950s and 1960s resulted, inevitably, in changes in education. Initial fragmentary responses in specific towns and cities in the 1960s were followed by more systematic developments of practice and policy through the 1970s and into the 1980s. These later developments progressively became more encompassing and more coherent in their application to schools. This book explores the policies, debates and controversies which have emerged as education has developed in response to the ethnic diversity and 'multicultural' nature of contemporary British society.

In attempting to capture the unique features of particular perspectives a succession of summary terms evolved as differing strategies for education followed each other: 'immigrant education', 'multicultural education', and 'anti-racist education' became the tags used to identify the distinctive features of the most dominant approaches up to the mid-1980s. Since then there have been further developments in educational practice, some stressing themes of social justice and equality, others, nationality and tradition.

The impetus for these changes in education originated from, and has been sustained by, a number of sources. From their arrival in the 1950s and 1960s, parents of ethnic minority pupils have expressed concern and taken action about the quality of education which schools have offered their children. From local and central government sources, statistical evidence has accumulated of differential patterns of educational performance linked with ethnic minority identity. Recent research into the interaction between teachers and pupils in schools and the criteria employed in streaming and banding has raised critical questions about the expectations and assumptions of teachers, and the ways in which these shape the careers of children and young people. Simultaneously, the evidence has mounted of the widespread experiences of discrimination encountered by black people in the workplace, in housing, in churches, and elsewhere.

This evidence has pointed directly towards the need for a complete reconsideration of schooling. No part of educational provision has escaped attention: staffing, the curriculum, resources, teaching strategies, links with the community, school routines for the use of names, school uniform, school meals, and other areas of normal school processes have all come under critical scrutiny. Moreover, it has been widely recognized that the educational task is not one just for urban multi-ethnic schools alone, but for all schools, including, and perhaps especially, those in isolated, remote, and predominantly or exclusively white communities.

No change of this magnitude comes without controversy. The controversies around the area of education for a multicultural society have been intense. They have involved battles of ideas waged through journals and newspapers and have included demonstrations and legal action by groups of parents against the decisions of local authorities. They have drawn the attention and engaged the participation of right-wing political extremists. In some cases the intensity of response has gone well beyond the boundaries of conventional debate and conflict in education.

The three major dimensions of this area of educational concern are identified above. They are the rapidity of change, the breadth of new educational policy and the intense nature of the debates and episodes in its evolution. Each of these dimensions poses considerable problems for those involved in education. Student teachers are daunted by the practical implications; they seek guidance on classroom strategies while remaining apprehensive about the controversies in the background. Meanwhile, teachers with considerable practical experience face the task of reviewing their practice in order to meet local authority guidelines but are anxious about 'tokenism'. Similarly, headteachers are concerned about potentially adverse reactions of parents and governors to any changes in the curriculum, assemblies, or school uniform regulations. Whatever the experience or seniority of those introducing change, there are likely to be misgivings in anticipation of counter-reaction to proposed changes.

This book's analysis of the development of educational policies for a multicultural society considers the major controversies in the field and addresses some of the concerns of students and teachers about teaching, schools and the community. Chapter 1 provides an overview of the development of cultural and ethnic diversity in Britain. Chapter 2 outlines the development of educational responses, including educational ideologies, central and local government policy development, and some of the implications for the school curriculum. Chapter 3 addresses the controversial issue of racism in society and in schools, including discussion of teaching about race and race relations and of ways in which schools have dealt with racist incidents. Chapter 4 summarizes four of the major episodes of conflict concerned with multicultural education in the 1980s. The final chapter raises questions about the effects on schools and the possibilities of continued progress in education for cultural diversity under the Education Reform Act and the National Curriculum.

Acknowledgements

This book has grown out of a period of active involvement in the development of educational policy and through teaching which has included initial teacher training and in-service education for teachers. I have learned a great deal from the contributions of teachers on in-service courses. I have gained considerably by thus working with people whose teaching skills and commitment to education have been exceptional. I have also had the opportunity to go into some of these teachers' schools where the enthusiasm of the pupils and the quality of their work are a delight. I would like to record my gratitude to these teachers. They know who they are.

Thanks are also due to the School Curriculum Development Committee who provided a grant for the purpose of investigating resources for teaching about race and race relations in schools. The effect of this project is particularly evident in Chapter 3, but it has also featured in the writing of other chapters. The project also involved Clive Billingham, Fabbeh Hussein, and Lesley McGuigan. I am grateful to them for sharing their expertise so openly.

I owe a particular debt to Fabbeh Hussein, whose approach to teaching in this controversial area, sharp perceptions, and wit have been a continuing resource. I should record my appreciation of those quiet conversations with my colleague Maurice Ziff which have helped me develop my understanding of the issues.

Finally, I would like to thank Frankie Todd for reading the

whole manuscript and for support and encouragement through the difficult stages of writing.

To Frankie, Zazie and Stefanie

1 The development of cultural and ethnic diversity in Britain

Changes in the key words of educational book titles published in the last three decades clearly signal the trends of the educational debates and policies which are the subject of this book. In the 1960s there was a change in the adjective describing the countries whence migrants came, from Colonial to Commonwealth. Subsequently, pupils in schools were transferred from 'immigrant' to 'ethnic minority' status. In the 1980s the theme of reports from a government committee of inquiry shifted, from 'West Indian children in our schools' (with its unmistakable 'us and them' connotations) to 'Education for All'. Later there was a counter-assertion from another source which used the title 'Education for Some'. By the late 1980s there was a reference to 'the interminable debate' in the title of a book about multicultural education, implying that the debates would never end.

There have also been changes in school practices, some reflecting adjustments to the outcomes of educational debate, and others contributing to new debates. For example, the welcome now offered to pupils and their parents in some schools is not exclusively in English; opportunities to participate in worship are provided in some schools for pupils whose religions are other than Christian; some school rules do not discriminate against the dress of ethnic minorities; and some school rules provide explicit procedures for challenging racialism in the classrooms, corridors and playgrounds.

These educational changes, and the controversies which are the central focus of this book, have their most obvious origins

1

in the post-war period. They are founded mainly upon the dynamics of responses to the migration and settlement in Britain of people from South Asia and the Caribbean from the 1950s until such migration was effectively reduced to a trickle by a series of legislative moves from the 1960s to the 1980s. However, there are good reasons to take account of the development of Britain as a culturally diverse society over a longer period than three or four decades. The history of migration and settlement of people to Britain, the processes of mutual adaptation, and the evolution of communities with roots in other countries spans many centuries.

While some migrations have led to changes in educational policy and shifts in educational debate, others have not. However, we can learn from the silences in debate, as well as the sounds. We can also gain understanding from the absence of policy initiatives as well as from their presence.

As a prelude to an overview of the educational debates and their implications for schools, the major purpose of this chapter is to review the processes of migration, settlement and the development of new communities in Britain. Although attention is concentrated on the last half century, European migrants and Britain's black population, some recognition is also given to Britain's cultural diversity over a much longer period of time. This review has relevance to diverse aspects of schooling, from the incorporation of materials about black people and community relations in the British history curriculum, to aspects of a school's links with the community, and to consideration of factors involved in the explanation of educational success and failure. However, this brief account can only serve as a series of small signposts to the educational issues which are taken up in greater detail later in the book.

Replays of 'the numbers game'?

Any review of migration and settlement in Britain which includes reference to reactions to migrant people, whether it spans the last three centuries or the last three decades, whether it focuses upon political refugees in an international context or the movement of gypsy trailers, inevitably picks up expressions of concern about numbers.

'The numbers game' is a phrase which has been used to refer to particular forms of debate about community change: forms of debate which implicitly carry moral dimensions and assumptions of the relative worth of different types of people. One recent parliamentary example occurred during discussions of the possibility of migration of people from Hong Kong to Britain. Similar arguments occurred in Parliament in earlier decades in discussion of migration to Britain from the new Commonwealth and Pakistan. A comment by Robert Moore, referring to discussion of the 1965 White Paper *Immigration from the Commonwealth*, illustrates the particular problems of this recurrent form of debate:

> The question of *numbers* became central to the black immigration debate.
>
> Once the debate is about numbers there are no issues of principle to be discussed, only *how many*? In being drawn into this discussion, liberals allowed themselves to be drawn onto racist ground because they were unable to argue about principles but had to accept the contention that coloured people were basically the problem. You can no longer argue that there is nothing wrong with black immigration or that it is positively a good thing. Similarly arguments about how much we benefited from black immigrants were very dangerous because they implied that people were entitled to certain rights only because they were useful. (Moore, 1975, p. 27)

The echoes from this numbers game can be heard in many places. There are educational equivalents in school staffrooms ('we don't have too many of these problems here'), in the comments made by some young people ('we offered them jobs, and now we're stuck with them') and in the fragmentary amalgamations of understanding and misunderstanding of some children ('they come here, crowding us, sir'). However,

3

the positive educational consequences of an understanding of the profiles of Britain's diverse communities are considerable. They include an awareness of materials which can be incorporated in the curriculum, the capacity to respond to pupils as individuals who also have a sense of collective identity (e.g., cultural, religious and social), and the power to participate in the development of a school ethos which achieves good educational standards.

There are grounds for anxiety about the misuse of data on ethnic minorities. However, the use of data about the ethnic identity of people does allow the monitoring of services to provide evidence about equality of treatment. The enumeration of the ethnic identity of respondents has now become a conventional part of the Labour Force Survey (after a long period of trial with different forms of questions). Students who apply for courses in higher education are expected to complete questions which identify their ethnic origin. Some employers include questions about ethnic identity on job application forms. This kind of recording has become part of the process of checking that unfair discrimination does not occur.

In education, information about a pupil's religion, language abilities, dietary preferences, etc., makes it possible for schools to take into account religious festivals (e.g., Jewish New Year, Eid, Diwali), design language awareness courses, provide appropriate food, and record pupils' names accurately. It is part of responding sensitively to the characteristics of children and young people and the communities to which they belong.

In the traditions: centuries of participation

The cultural, social and religious diversity of British society is not a new phenomenon. There have been changes, in the relatively short term (the last century), through migration and, in the longer term, through the continuous and normal development of lifestyles and the invention of social traditions.

Many features of 'British' culture incorporate the results of assimilating things from other societies, although we may not recognize the original components since our experience of the strands of contemporary custom can be seamless. For example, the components of our celebrations of Christmas include Christian and pre-Christian elements, traditions adopted from different countries, and religious and non-religious customs. Infant playground rituals with conkers use the seed of a tree which originated in Turkey. The great British diet of fish and chips uses the product of a plant from South America. The use of the Paisley print involved the adoption of a design brought from India and which has Persian origins.

Britain's links with Africa and Asia are particularly long-standing. An arresting sentence from a book by Peter Fryer clarifies this point:

> There were Africans in Britain before the English came here. They were soldiers in the Roman imperial army that occupied the southern part of our island for three and a half centuries. (Fryer, 1984, p. 1)

More generally, Fryer records that:

> Black people – by whom I mean Africans and Asians and their descendants – have been living in Britain for close on 500 years. They have been born in Britain since about the year 1505. (Fryer, 1984, p. xi)

Similarly, in a historical account of the presence of people from South Asia in Britain, Visram suggests:

> It is often forgotten that Britain had an Indian community long before the Second World War, and that the recent arrival of Asian people in Britain is part of the long history of contact between Britain and India ... Indian links with Europe go back 10,000 years. (Visram, 1986, p. 1)

These intercontinental contacts were not part of a series of happily crossed paths during gentle voyages of intellectual discovery and pleasant market trading. They were part of a process of expansion and quests for profit and for new territory, which established structures of relationships within and between societies that are still influential today. Put very directly:

> [t]he fact is that British history, from at least the sixteenth century, is inextricably woven with that of black people, through slavery, imperialism, and colonial domination. (Greater London Council, 1986, p. 4)

From the sixteenth century, black people arrived in England through extensions of the slave trade. Nevertheless, these origins did not consign the people involved to uniform or entirely predetermined social positions. Individual and collective action by black people enabled them to negotiate certain forms of participation in British society. There is evidence that black people lived as household servants, as courtesans and court entertainers. A painted panel of the 1570s shows Queen Elizabeth I with black musicians and dancers. Black women living in London in the eighteenth century worked as laundrymaids, seamstresses and nursemaids. Also in the eighteenth century, former slaves were active in the anti-slavery movement (Blackburn, 1988). In the nineteenth century there were a number of prominent black people in public life, including Mary Seacole, who nursed the sick and wounded during the Crimean War. Two MPs of Indian origin were elected to the House of Commons for London constituencies in the late nineteenth century (Dadabhai Naoraji 1892–5, and Sir M.M. Bhownagree 1895–1905). A third was elected in the 1920s (Shapurji Saklatvala 1922–3 and 1924–8) (Greater London Council, 1986).

As Pounce notes, 'about one third of the soldiers who fought on the British side in both [world] wars were from the Commonwealth. And about one eighth of them were black' (Pounce, 1985, p. 11). More than one million troops from India fought in World War I and about two and a half million fought in World War II.

The historical legacies of Britain's long-term contact with

continents other than Europe, and of the presence of black people in Britain, are quite pervasive. Their traces can be found in a range of institutions, in legislation, in English vocabulary, in street names, in the landscape, and in our diet. They may also be found in the values and attitudes of people who acquire their understanding of the world by growing up in what was once an imperial country. Nevertheless, there can be no doubt that these relatively hidden aspects of the presence of black people in British history are a challenge to many people. Moreover, with a few notable exceptions, the constructions of 'heritage' which appear in local museums, and which may be the only available basis for educational visits by schools, tend to represent British society as exclusively white, and its buildings, artefacts and technologies as emerging from purely local and indigenous energies.

Migration from Europe in the nineteenth and early twentieth centuries

Migration to Britain from Europe in the nineteenth and early twentieth centuries occurred as a result of a wide range of individual and societal circumstances. Some people were pushed by economic hardships and social, religious and political persecution. In many cases, the relative stability of Britain and the need for labour which accompanied economic expansion fostered the hopes and expectations of an improved standard of living. However, for some people the process of migration halted in Britain as a result of exhaustion of funds, and further destinations were not reached. The migration of people from Ireland, and Jewish people from elsewhere in Europe, has been particularly significant.

Irish migration
Irish migration to Britain has continued through several centuries with an expansion in the late eighteenth century. Some migration occurred on a seasonal basis, with participation as

7

'comers and goers' in the cycles of temporary, seasonal work which were available at the time (Samuel, 1973). It has been estimated that there were approximately 60,000 seasonal migrants in 1841. Some migration resulted in settlement in Britain, especially in those growing urban areas with a demand for semi-skilled and unskilled labour. In the middle decades of the nineteenth century, the official censuses of the population recorded increasing numbers of people of Irish origin living in England, Wales and Scotland. The 1841 census recorded more than 400,000 Irish people; the 1851 census (showing the impact of migration from the potato famine) 727,300; and the 1861 census recorded a peak of 806,000. Data recorded at intermittent intervals, with underlying classifications which assume a static population, inevitably fail to record some aspects of social processes. Census statistics underestimated the magnitude of the Irish population in Britain. Thus, as Miles and Solomos suggest:

> ... Census statistics included only people born in Ireland and therefore excluded those born to Irish parents in Britain. In taking this into account, one estimate of the total population of Irish origin in Scotland in mid nineteenth century doubled that suggested by the Census statistics. (Miles and Solomos, 1987, p. 77)

The major areas of settlement of Irish migrants were in London and the larger towns in Lancashire, with smaller concentrations in the West Midlands, Yorkshire and the north-east. Settlement in Scotland occurred mainly in the west, particularly around Glasgow. Miles and Solomos comment as follows:

> In purely numerical terms the number of Irish migrants to Britain has been far in excess of any other migration (for example, in 1961, there was a minimum of 1 million Irish-born people living in Britain, a statistic that does not include people of Irish descent, and yet there has been no state intervention to regulate this migration and settlement. The absence of legislation contrasts sharply with the response of the British state to migration from the Caribbean and the Indian sub-continent in the twentieth century,

demonstrating that numbers alone are not a sufficient determinant of state intervention. (Miles and Solomos, 1987, pp. 77–8)

Jewish migration

During the late nineteenth century it was estimated that there were about 60,000 Jewish people living in Britain, of whom less than half were migrants. The Jewish population was varied in terms of occupation – they were artisans, shopkeepers and merchants – and spanned the range of the socio-economic scale. Between 1870 and 1914 about 120,000 Jewish migrants entered and settled in Britain and by 1914 the Jewish population of Britain numbered about 300,000. There were economic and political reasons for migration. The effect of this migration is assessed by Miles and Solomos as follows:

> This migration changed the character of the Jewish population both economically and culturally. Most migrants originated in Eastern Europe, spoke Yiddish and had been engaged in various workshop trades or peddling . . . so that in Britain they constituted, at least initially, a culturally distinct section of the Jewish population and became concentrated in a limited range of workshop trades. (Miles and Solomos, 1987, p. 7)

During this period Britain was both an intermediate transit point (between Eastern Europe and the United States) and a place of settlement. The major places of settlement were London, Birmingham, Manchester, Leeds, and Glasgow. The main contributions to the local economies were, for example, through trades and businesses connected with boot- and shoe-making, dress-making and tailoring, and furniture-making.

European migration from the mid-twentieth century

Migration to Britain from elsewhere in Europe in the period immediately after the Second World War continued at significant levels. Migration from Ireland continued (there are estimates of between 70,000 and 100,000 arrivals between 1945 and 1951 and a total inward migration of 350,000 in the period from 1946 to 1959) (Castles *et al.*, 1984).

In addition, there were two schemes supported by the government which brought in significant numbers. First, provision was made for those people from Poland who were connected with the (non-Communist) Polish government and for the families and dependants of members of the Polish armed forces who had been fighting with the Allies. It was estimated in 1949 that about 128,000 Polish people were involved. Second, the European volunteer workers schemes brought in people from a number of European countries to help meet the labour shortages of the early post-war years. The schemes took in people from the Baltic states (Estonia, Latvia, Lithuania), Poland and Yugoslavia, Germany, Austria and Italy. Miles and Solomos (1987) argue that about 85,000 refugees were employed in the late 1940s as a result of these schemes. The volunteers were mainly single people, with limited civil rights, who were rarely allowed to bring other family members. Labour was needed in essential services such as agriculture, textiles, coal-mining and brick-making. Although employment was initially restricted to that which was specifically and contractually undertaken, it was announced in 1951 that once European volunteer workers had lived in Britain for three years, restrictions in their employment determined by the Ministry of Labour would be ended (Miles and Solomos, 1987).

There were measures of direct and indirect government assistance in the provision of help for Polish people. A number of voluntary groups, together with the Roman Catholic Church, also helped people to gain employment, obtain accommodation, and learn English.

Finally, renewable work permits were granted to about 100,000 Europeans, mainly from Italy in the 1950s and from Spain and Portugal in the 1960s (Castles *et al.*, 1984).

International divisions of labour

From the vantage point of the late 1980s, the broader and most far-reaching patterns of economic restructuring and social change in Europe connected with migration may be derived from the international movement of capital and plant, rather than of people. 'Mobile factories' (a phrase which has been used to symbolize the free movement of manufacturing around the globe to take advantage of cheap labour and low taxation) as well as mobile people have been the focus of state attention. In the mid-1980s at a time when there was comparatively little movement of people in and out of the UK, 40,000 manufacturing plants were opened in Third World countries (Gerhardt *et al.*, 1985). They included factories for the manufacture of textiles and clothing, computers, and electronic and other household goods. This transition played a role in the restructuring of European economies and was one element in the closing-down of manufacturing plants in Britain, thereby contributing to a surplus of some kinds of labour.

Only a few decades earlier, when manufacturing and public services were still rebuilding and expanding in the post-war period, problems of production were settled by the recruitment of labour. The recruitment of people to Britain in the immediate aftermath of the Second World War began a process which occurred simultaneously in other European countries. As summarized by Castles *et al.*:

From 1945 until the mid seventies, and most particularly during rapid expansion in the last 15 years of that period, the import of labour power was a marked feature of all advanced capitalist countries. Employers were looking for flexible labour units. Temporary foreign workers matched this requirement; they provided labour as and where required, without inflationary effects on wages or social expenditure. They were expected to remain only a few years, and to be easy to get rid of if no longer needed. Something like 30 million people entered the Western European countries as workers or workers' dependants in the post-war period, making

11

this one of the greatest migratory movements in human history. (Castles *et al.*, 1984, p. 1)

When expressed in minimal terms such as 'flexible labour units', which makes it clear that employers wanted workers, or 'units of labour for capitalist production', the demand is clear. However, the social and political dimensions of the phases of migration which followed the meeting of the demands for labour were not so simple:

> The character of the migrations has been complex and varied. They have included political refugees, black workers from colonies or former colonies, and 'guest workers' brought in from under-developed areas of Europe (Southern Europe, Finland, Ireland) often through organised labour recruitment. Each Western European country is a special case, where specific historical, demographic, economic and social conditions have shaped particular patterns of migration. (Castles *et al.*, 1984, p. 2)

It is these migrations of the mid-twentieth century and beyond which have triggered the development of recent educational policies. The phases of migration, settlement and community development unfolded gradually and each elicited educational responses. Castles *et al.* refer to 'three phases in the process of international migration which have led to the development of the new ethnic minorities' (Castles *et al.*, 1984, p. 11).

The first phase of labour migration involved mainly single people (predominantly but not exclusively male) and is typified as 'the phase of mass labour migration'. In general terms, this phase began about 1945 in Western Europe. There was a period of relatively gradual expansion in the 1950s, more rapid increases in the late 1960s and early 1970s and a rapid halt in 1973–4. Two countries were exceptions to this general description: West Germany and Britain. Britain cut migration abruptly in 1962 with the first of a series of immigration laws.

The second phase of the migratory process is labelled 'the phase of family reunification'. This phase began at a later stage and has been continuing as far as legislation allows, and at rates dictated by the procedures of the state. In the 1960s many migrants believed that they would eventually return to their countries of origin, and for them the phase of family reunification did not begin immediately. Subsequent immigration laws in Britain have prevented the unification of some families.

Castles *et al.* call the third and final stage 'the phase of permanent settlement and development of new ethnic minorities'. It is a phase in which new communities are established. These communities contain traditional elements and involve people linked by kinship and other elements. They also involve complex adaptations which may simultaneously indicate reactions to the new countries while promoting traditions originating in the old.

Migration from the New Commonwealth and Pakistan

Some migrants came to Britain with citizenship (granted under the Nationality Act 1948). They came from countries under the general umbrella title of 'New Commonwealth and Pakistan' and, while some came with the hope of finding work once they arrived, others filled jobs for which they had been specifically recruited before leaving their country. Fryer writes:

> British industry gladly absorbed them. In some industries the demand for labour was so great that members of the reserve army of black workers were actively recruited in their home countries. In April 1956 London Transport began recruiting staff in Barbados, and within 12 years a total of 3,787 Barbadians had been taken on. They were lent their fares to Britain, and the loans were repaid gradually from their wages ... in 1966 London Transport would begin to recruit in Trinidad and Jamaica too. The British Hotels and Restaurants Association recruited skilled workers in Barbados. And a Tory health minister by the name of Enoch Powell welcomed West Indian nurses to Britain. Willing black hands drove tube trains, collected bus fares, emptied hospital patients' bed-pans. (Fryer, 1984, p. 373)

At about the same time workers were recruited from Pakistan

to work in the textile mills in the West Riding of Yorkshire. The economic and micro-social changes of which this particular phase of migration was a part are made clear by Halstead in his discussion of the development of Bradford as a multi-ethnic city:

> As the East Europeans and other employees gradually left the textile mills for higher wages elsewhere, so the industry became more dependent on female labour. But when new machinery with greater productive capacity was introduced in the mid-1950s, it needed to be worked twenty-four hours a day to be economic. Women were not allowed by law to work the night-shift, but the single men who began to arrive in increasing numbers from India and Pakistan were seen by the employers as the solution to the problem. Some manufacturers began to advertise for labour in Pakistani newspapers ...
>
> For whatever reasons they came ... the Asians were welcomed by the textile manufacturers as they provided a cheap and compliant workforce which probably kept the industry competitive for several years longer than it would otherwise have been. (Halstead, 1988, pp. 8–9)

In numerical terms the migrants from India, Pakistan, the Caribbean and East Africa were less significant than migrants from Europe. In social and political terms they revealed clearly some of the dynamics, structures and mechanisms of British society and its institutions which were considered central to educational change in the 1980s. Before considering the current profiles of Britain's ethnic minority communities, it should be noted, for the purposes of summary, that the categorization of people as migrants filling particular positions in the labour market should not be taken to imply any uniformity of background, experience, educational level, or skill. As Castles *et al.* remark:

> While the popular image of work-permit holders from countries like Spain or Portugal, and of New Commonwealth migrants is of simple, uneducated peasants, the reality is different. These migrants do not form a homogeneous mass; they come from different his-

torical and political backgrounds, and from different classes within their own societies. For example, government language tests, financial guarantees and employment criteria effectively screened would-be Pakistani migrants and so ensured that only those with wealth and skills were allowed to migrate. In addition, recent research shows that some of the Indians who came to work in the foundries in the West Midlands were from the old colonial administrative class in the Punjab. Many who came from the ex-colonies had experience of the struggle for independence both within the labour movement and in the wider political arena. (Castles *et al.*, 1984, p. 42)

Britain's ethnic minority population now

Data on Britain's ethnic minority population from official sources are derived from the population censuses and from ongoing surveys such as the Labour Force Survey. Such data do not yield precise classifications and have been constructed in ways which do not reveal the complexities of ethnic, cultural or religious identity. There are sources of error within the data and it is thus common to aggregate the evidence from more than one year. With these reservations, what follows is a brief outline of the major estimates of Britain's ethnic minority populations, their socio-economic and some of their cultural characteristics.

Data derived from the Labour Force Survey, drawing upon the period 1984–6, give an overall total of ethnic minorities in Britain of 2.43 million people. This is approximately 4.5 per cent of the total population. Almost all (98 per cent) live in England and Wales. People of South Asian origin (Indian, Pakistani or Bangladeshi) comprise just over one-half of the total. People of Caribbean (West Indian, Guyanese) or African origin make up just over one-quarter. The growth of Britain's ethnic minority population from the 1950s through to the mid-1980s is shown in Table 1.1.

15

Table 1.1 *Estimated size of total ethnic minority population, Great Britain 1951–86*

	1951	1961	1981	1984–6
No. (thousands)	200	500	1,200	2,432
Percentage of total population	0.4	1.0	2.3	4.5

Source: C. Shaw (1988, p. 6, Table 2).

The composition of Britain's ethnic minority population as revealed by official statistics is shown in greater detail in Table 1.2. Whereas the inclusion of data on groups such as the Chinese and mixed races category gives some additional information, the underlying classification of 'white/non-white' underestimates the extent to which there are groups with distinctive cultural identities which are, in some senses, not part of a dominant homogeneous group. The Irish and Polish communities are examples from within the 'white' category. Similarly, the categorization of non-white by reference to national origin brings together people from, say, Caribbean islands which are quite different (and more than a thousand miles apart) and draws together people following different religious faiths into one group (e.g., Sikh and Muslim).

Almost half of the ethnic minority population (43 per cent) were born in the United Kingdom. Reflecting, as it does, some of the variations in migration and community development, this statistic conceals a wide range of variation. Nearly three-quarters of the mixed group, just over one-half of those

Table 1.2 *Population of Great Britain by ethnic group, 1984–6*

Ethnic group	Total	
	Thousands	Per cent
White	51,107	—
All ethnic minorities	2,432	100
West Indian	534	22
African	103	4
Indian	760	31
Pakistani	397	16
Bangladeshi	103	4
Chinese	115	5
Arab	66	3
Mixed	235	10
Other	119	5
Not stated*	691	—
All groups	54,230	—

*Official estimates of the people whose ethnic identity is recorded as 'not stated' are that they are almost exclusively 'white'.
Source: C. Shaw (1988).

categorized as West Indian, 42 per cent of those labelled Pakistani, just over one-third of Indian, just under one-third of Bangladeshis and about one in ten of those categorized as Arab, were born in the United Kingdom.

17

Table 1.3 records information about country of birth of the ethnic minority population in greater detail.

Table 1.3 *Population by ethnic group and country of birth (Great Britain, 1984–6 average)*

Ethnic group	Country of birth			
	UK	NCWP	Rest of the world	Number of people (thousands)
	%	%	%	
White	96	1	3	51,107
All ethnic minorities	43	47	7	2,432
West Indian	53	44	1	534
African	35	54	8	103
Indian	36	59	2	760
Pakistani	42	55	1	397
Bangladeshi	31	61	0	103
Chinese	24	50	26	115
Arab	11	2	85	66
Mixed	74	16	9	235
Other	28	34	34	119
All groups	93	3	3	54,230

Source: C. Shaw (1988).

One feature of a population which concerns educational planners, who need to forecast needs for the building of schools (or their closure) and the hiring (or firing) of teachers, is its age structure. The ethnic minority groups have a very young age structure compared with the white population. Whereas about one in three of the ethnic minority population (using mid-1980s data) is under 16, only one in five of the white population is under 16. Once again there is diversity within the different groups which affects the needs of educational provision in different localities. About half of the Pakistani, Bangladeshi and mixed groups are aged under 16 years.

Where do Britain's black people live?

A recurrent subsidiary theme of the account of migration to Britain in the nineteenth and twentieth centuries involves industrial development, with many, but not all, of the successive groups of migrants – European and non-European – moving to the same industrial locations. Ethnic minorities have never been randomly distributed: they settled where the work was. To a great extent, their descendants have remained in the towns of their parents, grandparents and great-grandparents (although some of the towns suffered severely in the economic recessions of the 1970s and, particularly, the 1980s). However, some, perhaps more commonly the self-employed, have taken part in the processes of migration within Britain.

Recent labour force survey data give relevant information about the populations of metropolitan areas. The highest proportions of black people live in Greater London and the West Midlands. Greater London has 57 per cent of Britain's West Indian or Guyanese population; 39 per cent of Indian; and 54 per cent of the Bangladeshi population. The population of Pakistani descent is distributed with 24 per cent in the West Midlands, 16 per cent in West Yorkshire, and 14 per cent in Greater London.

19

Although about two-thirds of the total population of the United Kingdom lives outside the metropolitan counties, less than one-third of the non-white population does so. Proportions for these major industrial areas range from about one in twenty to about one in seven (1983–85 averages, based upon the Labour Force Survey). More specifically, the percentage which the non-white group forms of the total population of the areas are:

Greater London 14 per cent
West Midlands 13 per cent
West Yorkshire 7 per cent
Greater Manchester 5 per cent

Insofar as some accounts of educational achievement draw upon social and economic factors external to the school, and some provision of funds for particular educational initiatives depends upon general features of the environment, it is relevant to mention that some of these areas have borne the brunt of the recession which was a part of the economic restructuring of the 1980s. Some were included in the list identified by the European Community as priority areas for grant aid to assist development from the Community's social fund. As areas which suffered most in the decline of Britain's manufacturing base through the 1970s and 1980s, they include communities which have coped with an accumulation of difficulties. Many are areas which expanded rapidly in the nineteenth century, and which have left a legacy of inadequate housing and poor environmental conditions. Some schools in these areas, whether old or relatively new, also display the symptoms of underinvestment in their decaying fabric.

Particular profiles

The patterns of settlement of ethnic minorities, which were partly derived from the needs of the economy, were also mediated by family and other social cultural links. Thus differ-

20

ent areas of the country now contain specific, unique clusters of communities. Between-town comparisons would show particular groups of Sikhs in one area, Muslims in another. Moreover, within towns there are spatial groups of people of similar background: Gujerats settling in one area of a large city for example, while Afro-Caribbeans settle in another. The aggregate population statistics therefore conceal the fact that Britain's cities have unique profiles of population and have developed differing educational needs.

The complex background to the determination of current educational needs can be demonstrated by reference to the city of Bradford. Bradford received a large number of migrants throughout the nineteenth and twentieth centuries from many countries. These included people from Ireland (more than 8 per cent of the population in 1851); people from Germany, mainly, but not only, Jews (estimated 300 in 1881); Russian and Polish Jews; and East Europeans in the post-Second World War period (European Volunteer Workers: Poles, Ukrainians, Latvians, Yugoslavs, Estonians, Belorussians and Lithuanians). People of East European origin comprised about 2 per cent of the city's population as recorded in the census of 1951. There were recruiting drives in the 1950s for the textile industry which brought in workers from Italy, Eire and Austria. Smaller groups which came in the post-war period were refugees from Europe – about 250 from Hungary in 1956 – and several hundred arriving from Vietnam in the 1980s (Halstead, 1988).

Halstead gives estimates of Bradford's black population, derived from local authority policy unit data, which show progressive increases over almost three decades. Estimates of numbers are as follows:

    1961 – 6,800
    1971 – 27,800
    1981 – 52,700
    1987 – 70,500

Family origins are as follows:

Pakistan	43,700
Bangladesh (mainly Sylhet)	2,600
India	16,000
West Indies	4,700
elsewhere in New Commonwealth (including East Africa)	3,500

The age structure of the ethnic minority population, referred to in general terms above, has specific implications for Bradford. In July 1983 the ethnic origins of the 87,250 children in Bradford schools were as follows:

- 77 per cent of UK/Eire origin
- 20 per cent of Asian origin, of whom 17 per cent were Muslim, 2 per cent Sikh, and 1 per cent Hindu
- 1.2 per cent of Afro-Caribbean origin
- 1.8 per cent of other origins, which include Western Europe, Eastern Europe and the Far East. (Halstead, 1988)

In the context of Britain's history, the arrival of a new group of migrants is as much part of a continuous tradition as it is a novelty. In terms of the relationships between the existing community and the newcomers it may involve similarity of purpose and experience which is as remarkable as any difference. The people who migrated to Britain from elsewhere came with the kinds of hopes of a better life for themselves and their families which are shared by the majority population. Moreover, Britain too has a tradition of migration, with individuals and families leaving to seek better conditions elsewhere, and then encouraging other family members to do the same. About four million more people migrated from Britain than arrived as immigrants in the sixty-year period from 1871 to 1931 (Booth, 1986). Thus there are towns in Australia, Canada and New Zealand with transplanted British kinship networks.

Community and cultural development

New communities bring new contributions. They also participate in the existing traditions of the societies which they join.

Carnivals, religious festivals, family and community celebrations, and fund-raising occasions for new hospital equipment, churches, community centres and schools are amongst the regular events in which there has been participation of Britain's ethnic minorities and their neighbours. Some features of ethnic community life are of relevance to pastoral care and school—community relationships; others are directly relevant to the curriculum and school procedures. Religious affiliation and language skills are particularly relevant to the development of educational policy: e.g. they impinge upon the school curriculum and on the provision of opportunities for religious worship.

Data on religious affiliation are not very precise but the growth of British membership of some of the major religions of the world is clear. *Social Trends* (Central Statistical Office, 1989), which takes its data from the *UK Christian Handbook* 1989/90 (MARC Europe), estimates that there are about 900,000 Muslims, 200,000 Sikhs, 150,000 Hindus, 109,000 Jews, and 220,000 followers of other religious faiths in the United Kingdom.

There are many non-standard varieties of English spoken in the United Kingdom, and there remain languages other than English (Welsh, Gaelic, Romany) which will continue as part of Britain's linguistic repertoire. Migration from other continents has introduced a number of bilingual pupils into schools and led to the extension of the range of language provision. The Swann Report on the numbers of pupils using a language other than English in five local education authorities illustrates this diversity (DES, 1985). The LEAs investigated were Bradford, Coventry, Haringey, Peterborough and Waltham Forest, and the survey was completed in 1981. The proportions of bilingual pupils were as follows:

Bradford 17.8 per cent
Coventry 14.4 per cent
Haringey 30.7 per cent
Peterborough 7.4 per cent
Waltham Forest 18.8 per cent

There were variations between the LEAs; the major languages in each area are summarized in Table 1.4.

Community diversity As the evidence on religions and languages suggests, Britain's ethnic minority communities are extremely diverse. Several ethnographic studies have emphasized this diversity (e.g., Ballard and Ballard, 1977; Bhachu, 1985; Pryce, 1986; A. Shaw, 1988.) They have also drawn attention to the traditions of migration and heterogeneity of communities in the countries from whence the migrants came. For example, Shaw concludes her introductory summary of migration from Pakistan to Britain, and in particular to Oxford, as follows:

> Pakistanis in Britain are from very different backgrounds in Pakistan, and include Panjabi groups, Mirpuris (or Azad Kashmiris) and the Pathans. Nevertheless, these groups share a history of internal migration through which they have sought to improve their lot, and in the past too, whether for military service or to colonize new land, the pattern of the migration has been based mainly on lines of kinship and village. The recent migration to Britain can therefore be viewed not as a radical departure from old ways or a search for a new life, but instead as a quest for a better life within the framework of existing cultural norms and values which are transported and adapted to new surroundings as the opportunities arise. The fact that through the process of chain migration migrants have been drawn selectively from particular villages also has important implications for the subsequent development of the Pakistani community in Britain, its social structure and its members' attitudes towards life in Britain. (A. Shaw, 1988, p. 28)

Some migrants came to Britain as part of a broader global chain involving several generations of migration. Bhachu's ethnographic account of East African Sikh settlers in Britain, in addition to providing a detailed picture of a particular community in Britain, also serves as a corrective to those who would tend to generalize about migrants to Britain of South Asian descent. East African Sikhs moved from urban East Africa to urban Britain. They were mainly public sector

Table 1.4 *Main Languages Reported in Five LEAs*

	Bradford	Coventry	Haringey	Peterborough	Waltham Forest
1. Total number of pupils recorded as using a language at home other than English	14,201	7,189	7,407	2,408	5,521
2. Total number of identifiably distinct languages reported	64	50	87	42	65
3. Most frequently reported spoken languages or language groupings as percentage of total to nearest whole number	Panjabi Urdu Gujerati Bengali Pushtu Italian Polish Hindi Chinese Creoles* Ukrainian	Panjabi 53 Gujerati 19 Urdu 9 Hindi 3 Italian 3 Bengali 3 Polish 1 Chinese 1 Creoles* 1	Greek 59 Turkish 16 Creoles* 7 Gujerati 3 Italian 2 French-based 2 Creoles 1 Bengali 1 Urdu 1 Panjabi Spanish Chinese French	Panjabi 34 Italian 15 Urdu 9 Gujerati 6 Chinese 6 Polish 4 German 3 Hindi 2 Creoles* 2 French 1	Panjabi 24 Urdu 24 Gujerati 18 Greek 12 Creoles* 4 Turkish 2 French-based 2 Creoles 2 Bengali 1 Chinese 1 Italian 1 Hindi 1 French 1
4. Total of 3 as cumulative % of 1	95%	93%	86%	90%	91%

*'Creoles' here means English-based and other non-French-based Creole languages.
Source: Swann Report (DES, 1985).

workers, technically skilled, from the central layers of a three-tier social hierarchy in the plural society of East Africa. They had considerable personal skills, together with financial and cultural resources. Bhachu writes:

> East Africans are therefore experienced migrants who had developed considerable community and technical skills prior to migration, and who also had powerful community ties which they have been able to reproduce in Britain since the late 1960s. They lack a strong orientation to a home country, and are settlers who combine facets of both progress and traditionalism in their settlement in the UK. (Bhachu, 1985, p. 2)

Bhachu refers to the reinforcement of ethnic identity in the British context. She describes the way in which adaptations to Britain involve the perpetuation of traditions; for example, with reference to family and marriage customs, arguing that:

> They are as much products of reactive pride in relation to racism from the majority community as of the values of a community settled in Africa during which time it developed a cohesive ethnic identity. (Bhachu, 1985, p. 162)

The dynamic aspects of culture, the adaptation of traditions and their development within a British context are common to Britain's ethnic minority communities. Moreover, the ways in which cultures are related to the power of a community, which is, in turn, linked with the community's relation to the structures of the dominant society, are illustrated in the detail of social networks and religious traditions.

The major implications for those in schools and education have been that it is necessary to be aware of the diversity and change amongst Britain's ethnic minorities. This diversity encompasses variations in language, religion, social status, and cultural values. However, as Bhachu concludes:

> In many respects, one has to deal with the universality of cultural traits. The problems of minorities are not exclusive to them e.g. the generation gap, truancy among school children and marriage breakdown, all exist as much among the majority indigenous Brit-

ish community as they do amongst minorities ... there is a large shared ground of common values and dilemmas existing among majority and minority alike. (Bhachu, 1985, p. 174)

This common ground of experience amongst children and young people who are also members of different churches and religions, or of different cultural or ethnic groups, is a potential resource for teachers. It provides opportunities through the curriculum and through classroom practice for the development of cohesion and mutual understanding within a context of recognition of difference.

The socio-economic position of ethnic minorities

The above references to diversity amongst ethnic minority groups have raised, indirectly, the issue of the socio-economic positions of Britain's ethnic minorities. Social class has a distinguished history as an explanatory factor in educational attainment. Some of the major discussions of the comparative educational attainment of white pupils and their ethnic minority counterparts have included consideration of social class position. An important part of these debates has been concerned with the extent to which ethnic minorities constitute an 'underclass'. An underclass is made up of those in the lowest-paid, least secure, most unpleasant jobs. Those in the underclass are particularly likely to suffer from unemployment. Characteristically, educational disadvantage is associated with the underclass. This review of the socio-economic situation of ethnic minorities briefly considers evidence relating to these debates.

The discussion is necessarily selective and does not include some of the important factors which relate to the socio-economic position of ethnic minorities. Collective action in economic, social, and political contexts is also an indicator of class relations. Yet there have been processes of exclusion which have reduced the potential of Britain's ethnic minorities from participation in, for example, trade union membership, leadership, or activity in professional groups. New forms of 'flexibility' in work, and the accompanying changes in the availability of part-time and temporary work and the expansion of home-working, are changing the map of Britain's class structure. Similarly, the increasing participation of women in the labour force is leading to modification of conceptions of the social class structure. Some of these changes have combined in their impact upon Britain's ethnic minorities: the interaction of class, gender, and race in stratified societies can have particularly strong effects on the creation of divisions.

This summary is based upon consideration of five major dimensions of the socio-economic profile of ethnic minorities:

1. The position of ethnic minorities in the labour market;
2. The unemployment situation of ethnic minorities;
3. The qualification levels of ethnic minorities;
4. The income levels;
5. The extent to which there are signs of change.

Ethnic minorities in the labour market

Labour Force Survey averages for the years 1985–7 estimate that about 4.6 per cent of the population of working people in Great Britain, i.e. about 1.55 million, were from ethnic minority groups. Each main ethnic minority group had a distinctive pattern of involvement in the labour market.

Ethnic minority groups constituted 7.6 per cent of the under-16 population, 4.6 per cent of the population of working age, and 0.8 per cent of the population of retirement age. Population projections, taking account of the age distributions of different groups, show a projected increase in the proportion of ethnic minority groups in the population of working age.

There are some patterns of variation in types of employment. Overall, 83 per cent of ethnic minority workers were employees, 15 per cent self-employed, and 2 per cent engaged on government training schemes. There were higher levels of self-employment among men of Indian and Pakistani/Bangladeshi origin (26 per cent and 22 per cent respectively). Among women, 7 per cent of those in employment were self-employed, a figure which included 12 per cent of those of Indian origin. In comparison with the white population, fewer were engaged in part-time work.

Distribution of work by industry is not the same as for the white population. There were 28 per cent of men from ethnic minority groups working in distribution, hotels, catering and repairs, whereas 16 per cent of the white male population worked in those categories. Ethnic minority men were relatively strongly represented in transport and communications and health services. Relatively few worked in construction or agriculture. Ethnic minority women were more likely to work in the health services and in parts of the manufacturing sector than their white counterparts.

Data on the overall occupational distribution of white and ethnic-minority workers show broadly similar proportions of males in non-manual and manual occupational groups (46 per cent and 54 per cent respectively). However, there were variations among the different ethnic minority groups. These differences are particularly marked when the hierarchy of occupations is considered: about one in four West Indian men and about one in three Pakistani/Bangladeshi men were non-manual workers, whereas over half those of Indian or other origins were non-manual workers. The figures on managerial and professional occupations indicate that 12 per cent of West Indian, 42 per cent of Indian, and 26 per cent of Pakistani/Bangladeshi working men are classified in those categories. Amongst manual occupations, West Indian workers show the highest proportion; 30 per cent of West Indian males are engaged in craft manual work (*Employment Gazette*, 1988).

The data also reveal other differences in patterns of employment in terms of the occupational hierarchy. Thirty-five per cent of the white male population is in the professional and employee management category compared with only 12 per cent of West Indians. Brown reported that 3 per cent of the white male population is in the unskilled manual category compared with 12 per cent of the Bangladeshi, 9 per cent of the West Indian, and 8 per cent of the Pakistani population. Consideration of the data on females reveals that only 1 per cent of West Indian women are in the professional employee/ management category, whereas the figures for white and Indian women are 7 per cent and 5 per cent respectively (Brown, 1984).

Turning to women's occupational distribution, the data show a higher proportion of the white population than of ethnic minority groups in the non-manual rather than manual occupations. Indian women are more likely than others to be in skilled manual work. The numbers involved in some of these categories are very small and care must be taken not to generalize. The recorded rate of participation in economic activity for women in the Pakistani/Bangladeshi group is 18 per cent, whereas that for Indian women is 55 per cent. The figure for economic participation of white women is 68 per cent.

Higher rates of self-employment are found among Indian/ Pakistani and Bangladeshi males than among the white population (16 per cent compared with 11 per cent). The highest rate of self-employment is among Indian males (18 per cent) (Central Statistical Office, 1989, p. 72).

Educational and occupational qualifications

In general terms, white people of working age are more likely to have qualifications of some kind than are people from ethnic minority groups, with the biggest difference occurring in the over-45 age band. Once again there are differences between ethnic groups: those of Pakistani/Bangladeshi origin are least likely to possess qualifications (62 per cent of men and 76 per cent of women do not have formal qualifications). West Indian men also tended to be less well-qualified than other ethnic minority categories. Younger people are better qualified than their older counterparts, reflecting different life histories of participation in the educational system.

Income

A Policy Studies Institute report (Brown, 1984) records significant inequalities in incomes, as Table 1.5 reveals.

Table 1.5 *Gross median weekly earnings of full-time employees by regions*

Region	Whites	Blacks
England and Wales	£128.90	£110.20
North-West	141.50	98.60
Yorkshire/Humberside	116.20	103.70
West Midlands	130.20	105.90
East Midlands	135.40	96.00
South-West	129.20	107.50
South-East (excluding London)	126.90	115.20
London	129.90	118.70

The disparities of income between white people and ethnic minorities do not disappear when job levels are held constant (see Table 1.6).

Unemployment

Combined Labour Force Survey data for 1985–7 show higher official unemployment rates for the ethnic minority population than for the white population. This pattern remains present even when educational levels are taken into account. The lowest unemployment rates are amongst the white population with A-level or higher qualifications: 3 per cent for males and 5 per cent for females. The highest unemployment rates are amongst the Pakistani/Bangladeshi male population with no

31

Table 1.6 *Gross median weekly earnings of full-time employees, by job level*

Job level	Male		Female	
	White	Asian/ West Indian	White	Asian/ West Indian
Professional, employer Manager	£184.70	£151.80	£106.80	£122.10
Other non-manual	135.80	130.40	81.70	86.00
Skilled manual	121.70	112.20	66.90	74.40
Semi-skilled manual	111.20	101.00	66.50*	72.40*
Unskilled manual	99.90	97.80		
All	129.00	110.20	77.50	78.50

*Semi-skilled and unskilled manual categories, combined.
Source: Ohri and Faruqi (1988), amended from Brown (1984).

qualifications (31 per cent). The overall unemployment rates from these data were: white, 11 per cent; West Indian 21 per cent; Indian, 16 per cent; Pakistani/Bangladeshi 29 per cent; other, 17 per cent. This latter category includes African, Arab, Chinese, other stated and mixed respondents (Central Statistical Office, 1989, p. 81).

As implied above, there are variations by age, gender and qualifications but higher unemployment amongst ethnic minorities remains when these factors are taken into account. The highest rates of unemployment are amongst the Pakistani/Bangladeshi communities, and amongst 16- to 24-year-olds in each of the main ethnic minority groups. The differentials in unemployment rates for young people are significant. The unemployment rates for the differing categories of 16- to 24-year-olds in 1987 were 16 per cent white; 30 per cent ethnic minority (32 per cent West Indian/Guyanese; 25 per cent Indian; 37 per cent Pakistani/Bangladeshi).

There have been some fluctuations in the trends. For example, in each year between 1984 and 1986, the unemployment rate for the ethnic minority groups was nearly twice that for the white population, but in 1987 it declined in relative terms to a level two-thirds above that for the white group.

Generally speaking, the unemployment pattern for ethnic minorities reflects the regional distribution of unemployment. However, with some minor variations, the ratio of ethnic minority to white unemployed in the different regions is about 2:1.

The absence of change in the socio-economic position of migrant groups

In the third PSI report Brown (1984) concludes that there has been little change since the 1950s and 1960s in the socio-economic position of black people. Rather than ascending the occupational hierarchy, their positions in the lower levels of the labour market had been sustained, with accompanying lower levels of income. The evidence from those cities where there have been black settlements for a long time, e.g., Liverpool, suggests that this static situation is not one only of recent decades but may be reproduced over many future generations.

Conclusions

The participation of black people in British society has a long history. Recent patterns of migration and settlement have included groups from Europe as well as ethnic minorities from South Asia and the Caribbean. The cultural patterns and the socio-economic features of ethnic minorities who have come to Britain in the post-war years are diverse. However, there is some evidence that there has been little change in their socio-economic profiles and that there are some marked differences between black and white people in terms of their experiences in the labour market. Each of these aspects of Britain's multi-ethnic society has relevance to schools. Chapter 2 considers the major ways in which the educational system has responded to the post-war changes in Britain's population.

2 The development of educational policies for a multicultural society

This chapter describes the evolution and development of educational provision and policies from central and local government and considers their effects upon schools. Inevitably, given the scale and complexity of new initiatives in education for a multicultural society, this includes piecemeal responses by local authorities or schools and more systematic direction from central government. It includes discussion of developments in multi-ethnic and predominantly white areas since, although the trends of multicultural education may have been started in multi-ethnic areas, the tasks of education for a multicultural society are not exclusively theirs. It includes consideration of the processes of policy implementation, and the levers and mechanisms of change as well as analysis of policy documents.

There are four main strands to the argument which follows. First, some of the general educational issues and general educational ideologies relevant to multicultural education are considered. Second, an overview is offered of some of the major policy developments from central government. Third, local government policies are analysed with reference to the processes of policy development and their implementation. Finally the school is considered, with reference to aspects of the curriculum.

Ideologies and orientations

Schools are not institutions which can solve all of the problems of the outside world, but their role as part of society is important and questions about their general objectives can be legitimately raised. One of the major questions about schools as agents of change is concerned with schools as places which, both directly and indirectly, are working towards the assimilation of ethnic minorities. Put a different way, the issue becomes one of the extent to which schools facilitate pluralism in society. This raises questions as to what is meant by assimilation and pluralism.

Assimilation

It is common to find that use of the term 'assimilation' implies a straightforward, one-way process of a minority group adapting to a majority culture. This is reflected in Giddens's definition of assimilation as 'the acceptance of a minority group by a majority population, in which the group takes over the values and norms of the dominant culture' (Giddens, 1989, p. 735). Although this hints at a two-way process, the emphasis is upon change within the minority group. Moreover, it appears that the minority passively change while the majority hold the power of tolerance or rejection, ultimately demonstrating acceptance of the assimilated minority. Giddens elaborates as follows: 'assimilation, meaning that immigrants abandon their original customs and practices, moulding their behaviour to the values and norms of the majority' (Giddens, 1989, p. 271). However, there are reasons to raise questions about the extent to which processes of assimilation are ever entirely one-way and indeed to analyse the situation in order to consider different elements of assimilation and features of the process which are related to time.

These complexities of change and adaptation during the assimilation process are considered by Banton, who remarks:

> ... it is a matter of common observation that cultural change among immigrants proceeds more rapidly in respect of behaviour that helps them earn a living, like learning a language, than in their private domestic lives. The implication of a uniform process of change is misleading, as is the failure to acknowledge that the

receiving group undergoes change in absorbing the other. (Banton, 1983, p. 144)

As well as asserting that there are processes of change on both sides of the ethnic boundary, Banton draws attention to the complexity of change. He points out that

> It is now widely accepted that a conception of assimilation as a unitary process is misleading. ... The adoption by immigrants of majority practices may give an appearance of change but underlying values may not have altered. Moreover, the majority itself is divided by socio-economic status, regions, life-styles and perhaps by ethnicity. Social life in the different sectors, of work, schooling, home and religion, may be compartmentalized so that it becomes difficult to identify the group or practices in the majority society to which the minority may be expected to assimilate. It is customary to ask to what extent a minority is assimilated, but the question can also be asked of the majority. (Banton, 1983, pp. 145–6)

Aspects of these two-way processes are apparent in schools, with young white people enjoying Afro-Caribbean music, emulating the hairstyles of their ethnic minority friends, and even speaking patois.

In contrast to the modelling of one group by another there are also, commonly, some processes of differentiation. As Banton records, 'A group that is assimilating to the minority in certain respects may increase its differentiation in others' (Banton, 1983, p. 148). Such differentiation may be particularly asserted in generations of ethnic minorities who are born in a foreign country, rather than by their parents, who migrated. For example, some people who migrated to Britain in the 1960s argue that their children will not submit to some of the racialism which they suffered and instead will challenge whatever hostility they encounter. Thus the wearing of turbans by young Sikhs (Ballard and Ballard, 1977) and the emphasis of some religious customs and family traditions (Bhachu, 1985) are indicators of the extent to which ethnic minority groups of different generations may respond in ways which emphasize

37

their difference from the majority. The renewal and reconstruction of ethnic identity is one part of the pattern of relationships between the majority and the minority.

Pluralism

If it is accepted that the majority of society is not in itself homogeneous and that the processes of adaptation are not uniform, this may involve the heightening of differentiation as well as change by both the majority and minority, thus making the nature of society as a *pluralist* society an issue. In general terms, and evidently drawing upon cross-cultural evidence, a plural society is defined by Giddens as 'a society in which several ethnic groupings coexist, each living in communities or regions largely separate from the others' (Giddens, 1989, p. 746).

The notion of a pluralist society has often been used in debates about multicultural education, either as an ideal or as a working assumption (DES, 1985; Verma *et al.*, 1989). Its use in educational contexts has been separate from its use in social anthropology and political analysis. It is now, perhaps, a tradition in political analysis to use the term with implicit or explicit recognition of the extent to which apparent pluralism conceals the operations of power which reproduce substantial inequalities in society (Lukes, 1974). Certainly the mere presence of identifiably different groups within a society is no guarantee of equal participation as citizens, equal life-chances, or equality of opportunity. Similarly, the presence of ethnic minorities in schools does not eliminate processes of unfair discrimination in, for example, the banding or streaming process. Although the educational use of the term pluralism has symbolic significance, particularly as a challenge to those who assert ideas of a dominant and unitary British culture, it may be used in contexts which fail to illuminate the realities of power in education (Sachs, 1986).

Assimilation and pluralism assume particular significance as identifiable features in the mapping of general approaches to education in a multicultural society. There are now not only a number of broad approaches which are distinctly labelled, but also several alternative ways of classifying these approaches. It is these global perspectives, reflecting educational ideologies, and generally stated purposes and objectives which are now considered.

Approaches to education in a multicultural society

Educational policies have altered following changes in the composition of British society. These policies have incorporated knowledge of how a multi-ethnic society works and how schools influence young children and young people. There are relatively clear differences between the various approaches to multicultural education. However, there is no consensus on how many distinctive approaches have evolved. There are ways of classifying these general approaches which demonstrate how each approach is part of a more general ideology, which includes views of the purposes of education and how specific conceptions of educational problems link with more general models of British society. The relationship between these elements is explained by Mullard as follows:

> ... all the racial forms of education that have scurried across the landscape of educational history over the last twenty years – immigrant, multiracial, multicultural, multi-ethnic, poly-ethnic, and anti-racist education – stand and face each other in a relatively similar way. This is so because they all draw upon different or slightly different perspectives and perceptions of socio-educational reality and objectives. In short, they all evoke positions on the nature of the social and educational; they all invoke their own set of decisions in respect to (preferred) definitions of the problem in society and education and hence (preferred) conceptions of social and educational objectives. (Mullard, 1984, p. 7)

In the course of drawing attention to the network of ideas integrating conceptions of society with those of education, Mullard has used six labels to identify qualitatively different forms of education: immigrant, multi-racial, multicultural, multi-ethnic, poly-ethnic and anti-racist. Some of these he links with particular decades. He suggests, for example, that immigrant education was the approach of the 1950s and 1960s; multi-racial education 'surfaced in the mid-1960s'; whereas multicultural education developed in the 1970s. Mullard also uses a distinction which divides these six types into two. He argues that whereas the first five are implicitly or explicitly racist, the final approach is not. A distinctive feature of Mullard's analysis is that it is based upon a generative model of the underlying mechanisms and structures of capitalist society. This model draws connections between changes in the global economy (which affect the movement of people and industry) and changes in the education system.

New educational ideologies do not grow out of the air: they commonly involve transformations of earlier concerns, and may require only minor adaptations of educational discourse. The connections between specific educational problems and the approach to education for a multicultural society are apparent in Banks's typology of multicultural education (Banks, 1986). His typology distinguishes approaches to multicultural education according to their major assumptions, goals and consequences (where appropriate) for school programmes and practices. It is part of a model of ethnic and cultural development and incorporates examples from several societies.

There are ten categories in Banks's model, each one functioning to emphasize specific aspects of educational policy or explanations of educational achievement. The labels for each category are: ethnic additive, self-concept development, cultural deprivation, language, racism, radical, genetic, cultural pluralism, cultural difference, and assimilationism. Many of these categories (together with their corresponding assumptions, educational goals, and school practices) are not, of course, specific to the education of ethnic minorities. They are also part of the consideration of inequalities in education as related to, say, social class or rural deprivation.

The category systems constructed by Mullard and Banks illustrate different ways in which multicultural education has been seen in the context of aspects of global change and how it connects with other educational ideologies. There are other classifications which use other underlying principles. Kirp (1979) emphasizes two major approaches, characterized according to whether they are 'racially explicit' or 'racially implicit', in a discussion which contrasts the UK with the USA. However, Sleeter and Grant (1987), in a review of multicultural education in the United States, distinguish five approaches. These are:

1. Teaching the culturally different ('trying to equip people of color more successfully with the knowledge and skills to compete with Whites' (p. 426));
2. Human relations ('to help students of different backgrounds communicate, get along better with each other, and feel good about themselves' (p. 426));
3. Single group studies ('lessons or units that focus on the experiences and cultures of a specific group, such as an ethnic group' (p. 428));
4. Multicultural education, emphasizing the positive aspects of cultural diversity and equality of opportunity, and
5. 'Education that is multicultural and social reconstructionist' which 'prepares young people to take social action against social structural inequality' (p. 434).

Elements of each of these five approaches are synthesized in some of the policies developed by local education authorities in Britain.

A model of greater simplicity, which is firmly rooted in a British context and which has been used extensively in inservice education for teachers, maps three approaches and is reproduced below. To test your awareness of the different approaches, the following task is recommended. Copy the page, cut out the 15 statements (separating them from the column headings), shuffle them, and then sort the statements in whichever way seems most appropriate. Also consider the extent to which you agree or disagree with the statements.

41

Issues and controversies in the Swann Report: a model

A	B	C
Immigrants came to Britain in the 1950s and 1960s because the laws on immigration were not strict.	Ethnic minorities came to Britain because they had a right to and because they wanted a better life.	Black people came to Britain, as to other countries, because their labour was required by the economy.
Immigrants should integrate as quickly as possible with the British way of life.	Ethnic minorities should be able to maintain their language and cultural heritage.	Black people have to defend themselves against racist laws and practices, and to struggle for racial justice.
There is some racial prejudice in Britain, but it's only human nature, and Britain is a much more tolerant place than most other countries.	There are some misguided individuals and extremist groups in Britain, but basically our society is just and democratic and provides equality.	Britain is a racist society, and has been for several centuries. Racism is to do with power structures more than with the attitudes of individuals.
It is counter-productive to try to remove prejudice – you can't force people to like each other by bringing in laws and regulations.	Prejudice is based on ignorance and misunderstanding. It can be removed by personal contacts and the provision of information.	Prejudice is caused by, it is not the cause of unjust structures and procedures. It can be removed only by dismantling these.
There should be provision of English as a Second Language in schools, but otherwise 'children are all children, we should treat all children exactly the same' – it is wrong to notice or emphasise cultural or racial differences. Underachievement is caused by home background and culture.	Schools should recognise and affirm ethnic minority children's background, culture and language ... celebrate festivals, organise international evenings, use and teach mother tongues and community languages, teach about ethnic minority history, art, music, religion, literature.	Priorities in education are for there to be more black people in positions of power and influence – as heads, senior teachers, governors, education officers, elected members; and to remove discrimination in the curriculum, classroom methods and school organisation; and to teach directly about equality and justice and against racism.

(Richardson, 1985, p. 13)

This model of issues and controversies summarizes three general approaches to education in a multicultural society. The five rows in the model demonstrate the different interpretations of the history of post-war migration, the major task of adaptation to British society of the migrants, the nature of British society, the significance of prejudice and the educational issues. Although the model shows the distinctiveness of the different approaches, it does not attempt to provide an explanation for educational change.

As in any map, there is in the model an element of simplification, of generalization and of heightened contrasts. Nevertheless, the statements in each section, broad as they are, capture the relationships between three major perspectives and the essential features of their discourse. For example, whereas column A refers to 'immigrants', column B refers to 'ethnic minorities' and column C speaks of 'black people'. Moreover, the context of references to 'immigrants' in column A makes it clear that these are not references to all the people who migrated to Britain, but to those in particular from the New Commonwealth and Pakistan, or even more specifically to those from the Caribbean, India and Pakistan. In other words it is a coded reference based upon a colour distinction.

The existence, or representation, of prejudice and discrimination is identified differently in each column. Whereas column A speaks only of attitudes, referring to 'prejudice' and then reducing this to a matter of personal preference, there is a contrasting approach in column C. Column C focuses upon laws, practices and procedures – in a word, structures – which are identified historically as the origin of attitudes which are 'prejudiced'. This implies that people's attitudes are derived from the practices of the social institutions in which they participate.

The educational objectives of a multicultural society differ between each of these approaches. Clearly, the first stresses British traditions and identifies educational problems in association with the cultures and languages of black people. In effect, black people are defined as an educational problem. The second offers a kind of cultural pluralism, with its references to the provision of knowledge and understanding of ethnic minority cultures and the celebratory approach. The third approach stresses equality and justice, the unity of black people in the face of discrimination within British society, urges challenges to racism, and suggests procedures to ensure equality in teaching and within schools.

The question arises about how to label these perspectives. True to its origins as a basis for open discussion by teachers, the model above has been reproduced with relatively neutral letters identifying the columns. A set of labels is offered by Houlton (1986). His headings and subheadings, moving from left to right, are: 'Assimilation: what most people still believe'; 'Multiculturalism: what well-meaning liberals believe', and 'Anti-Racism: what genuine anti-racists believe'. The headings typify the approaches and subheadings expose some of the undercurrents of social and political labelling which are a part of education.

There is a hidden dimension of time in this model. Perhaps it is sufficient to say at this stage that column A brings together an orientation which encapsulates the earliest educational responses to black people in Britain in the 1950s and 1960s. Column B's pluralist 'multiculturalist' approach developed at a later stage. Column C draws out some of the major elements of anti-racist approaches of the early and mid-1980s. The correlations between Richardson's and Mullard's models are clearly evident.

The representation of educational ideologies in Britain in this way has become conventional, to the extent that some local education authority policies provide a brief resumé of phases of development. Some of these identify four, rather than three, phases. They identify, say, assimilationist, integrationist, multiracial, and anti-racist approaches. However, if the earlier discussion about the issues of assimilation and integration are kept in mind, there is little difficulty in outlining four approaches rather than three. Moreover, the evidence that each stage existed in a distinctive way is sometimes minimal. As an example, the Leeds City Council's justification for an anti-racist policy includes the following:

In the past, responses to issues of race and education have been based upon the perspectives of assimilation (Immigrant Education or 'Deficiency Model'), integration (Multi-Racial Model) and cultural diversity (Multi-Cultural Education Model). In the 50s and 60s Immigrants' Education or 'Deficiency Model' was developed in response to the presence of non-British born pupils and students. The problem was seen as existing in the lack of spoken and written English and knowledge of British life and cultures. Once these deficiencies were overcome, it was assumed that these young people would be assimilated into the British education system. The Multi-Racial Model which emerged in the late sixties and early seventies emphasised the reality of Britain as a multi-racial society in which black communities were seen as disadvantaged. Through this model, resources were sought to integrate the black pupils and students into the education system without the abandonment of their culture. The Multi-Cultural Model became the most dominant educational response (in the seventies) to the presence of black people in Britain. In this model, there is a concern to provide opportunities for cultural and language maintenance and introduction of cultural and religious festivals in schools having a large number of children from the ethnic minority communities . . . [A]ll the approaches mentioned above have been found to be inadequate . . . The implication of all these models is that the existence of the black people and their culture is the problem . . . In fact, the real response to race and education should be based on equality – with central attention being given to racism and to measures to unlearn and dismantle racism. (Leeds City Council, 1987, pp. 2–3)

As time goes by, any classification of approaches to education for a multicultural society will need additional phases in order to accommodate new ideologies. From the middle and late 1980s, the Education Reform Act, the National Curriculum, and the ideology of some Conservative local authorities are jointly entering new phases of educational development. This is not predictable from the typologies described above. These typologies are, inevitably, reflections on the past. They are also static, neither indicating why change occurred nor how it occurred. Questions remain as to what extent the ethnic minority communities have prompted change through their increasing participation in local politics; how much the disturbances in Brixton, Toxteth and Handsworth contributed to educational change; whether these new policies are leading to fundamental changes in schools or whether they are merely cosmetic.

Some of the statements found in past local education authority documents imply a kind of progress through an educational consensus. Moreover, this model of progress is represented as leading us towards a clear destination. History will not repeat itself in the 1990s, but there may be an occurrence of the circular as authoritarian ideologies of assimilation, stressing the adaptations to be made by ethnic minorities, combine with centrally controlled educational measures to suppress earlier initiatives in multicultural and anti-racist education.

Whatever the external events, there has been considerable discussion of the educational merits of the differing approaches to education. Some of the key discussions are summarized below, with particular reference to the relationship between the three broad approaches outlined in the model above.

The limitations of liberal 'monocultural' education

What are the consequences of an approach to education which is defined in traditional terms, i.e. a form of education that stresses British traditions and perspectives without reference to the cultural diversity of Britain or consideration of other perspectives? Parekh (1986) typifies a traditional view of education as having three objectives:

> First, it aims to cultivate such basic human capacities as critical reflection, imagination, self criticism, the ability to reason, argue, weigh up evidence and to form an independent judgement of one's

own ... Second it aims to foster such intellectual and moral qualities as the love of truth, openness to the world, objectivity, intellectual curiosity, humility, healthy scepticism about all claims to finality and respect and concern for other ... Third it aims to familiarize the pupil with the great intellectual, moral, religious, literary and other achievements of the human spirit. (Parekh, 1986, p. 19)

Parekh describes this view of education as 'intellectually persuasive' but seriously flawed and 'sociologically naïve'. Education occurs in a particular historical, social and cultural context, and the dominant culture has a major effect. This effect, he argues, is realized through the educational structure and organization, through the curriculum content (which is selective), and through teaching methods. Parekh thus challenges the claim that the traditional view of education is liberating or even liberal, arguing that it is a relatively narrow education in 'the kind of culture that has become dominant in the West since the eighteenth century' (Parekh, 1986, p. 20).

The effects of such a monocultural education upon the child of the dominant culture are damaging. Parekh makes five points:

First, it is unlikely to awaken his curiosity about other societies and cultures because he is not exposed to them at all or because they are presented in uncomplimentary terms, or both ... Second, mono-cultural education is unlikely to develop the faculty of imagination ... Third, mono-cultural education stunts the growth of the critical faculty ... Fourth, mono-cultural education tends to breed arrogance and insensitivity ... Fifth, mono-cultural education provides a fertile ground for racism. Since a pupil knows very little about other societies and cultures he can only respond to them in terms of superficial generalizations and stereotypes. (Parekh, 1986, pp. 23–4)

Such an education will also have deleterious effects upon the black child, creating a tendency towards feelings of inferiority and worthlessness, and diminishing the quality of relationships with the child's own people. Thus a monocultural education 'damages and impoverishes all – black or white' (Parekh, 1986, p. 26).

Multicultural education is described by Parekh as an attempt to release a child from the confines of the 'ethnocentric strait-jacket'. Moreover:

> It does not cut off a child from his own culture: rather it enables him to enrich, refine and take a broader view of it without losing his roots in it.
>
> The inspiring principle of multi-cultural education then is to sensitize the child to the inherent plurality of the world – the plurality of systems, belief, ways of life, cultures, modes of analyzing familiar experiences, ways of looking at historical events and so on. (Parekh, 1986, p. 27)

Multiculturalism and the spectre of relativism

When confronted by accounts of multicultural education some critics, rather than seeing freedom and inspiration, enrichment of understanding and the splendid diversity and resourcefulness of different civilizations, have not been impressed. Rather, they have had visions which have included social disintegration (Honeyford, 1988), the collapse of objective standards (Palmer, 1986), threats to the absolutes of morality (Scruton, 1986), and incoherence (Wilson, 1986; DeFaveri, 1988).

Arguments about objectivity and relativism have a long history and show similar characteristics across a range of concerns including scientific knowledge, cross-cultural understanding and ethics (Hollis and Lukes, 1982). One common ploy in arguments against multiculturalism is to define it as a 'relativist' position in some extreme form and to demonstrate that it is self-refuting. The failings of those who support some form of relativism may also be typified in extreme terms of mental disorder; e.g., Wilson (1986) writes: 'Relativism is at root a kind of despair, a form or symptom of autism produced by loneliness and lack of communication' (p. 96).

As an example of this type of argument, consider DeFaveri (1988); he begins an article about multiculturalism as follows:

Much of the recent literature on multiculturalism is unfortunately dominated by an untenable relativism. Many writers assume that there is no rational way to compare the worth of cultures and, as a supposed consequence of this assumption, all cultures are to be respected equally.

This is silly. Imagine two cultures, otherwise the same, but one of which is racist. Why assume they are equally meritorious, or equally worthy of respect, or that there are no standards by which they can be compared? Why continue to assume that no transcultural judgements are possible and that there are no acts which, while acceptable within a particular culture, are nevertheless crimes against humanity? (DeFaveri, 1988, p. 4)

DeFaveri then quotes a comment by Rivlin (1973):

One of the most difficult words for people to understand when they look at various cultures or sub-cultures is *different. Different* means *different*; it does not mean *better than* or *worse than*. This whole-hearted acceptance of one's own culture and of other people's culture is basic to the development of a sense of cultural pluralism.

This is followed by a charge:

Rivlin's extreme relativism is not a coherent position. If what he says is true, his claim must also apply to what he himself says. Thus if he says that any utterance is nothing other than a reflection of the values of one's culture, and no culture is better or worse than any other, then what he says is no better or worse than what is said by someone whose culture demands that he say the exact opposite of what Rivlin is saying. He is in effect both asserting and denying the same thing and therefore is saying nothing of any importance to anyone. (DeFaveri, 1988, p. 4)

The 'relativism is self-refuting' argument may appear to have force: indeed, it is commonly applied with considerable force. Nevertheless, Rorty's suggestion that these argumentative ploys 'only work against lightly-sketched fictional characters' or that

49

they 'are adopted to make *philosophical* points – that is moves in a game played with fictitious opponents, rather than fellow-participants in a common project' (Rorty, 1982, p. 167) certainly applies to some of the charges about relativism. An argument which is more to the point is that of Bhaskar (1989). Bhaskar argues that the 'relativism is self-refuting' argument is itself easily refuted. He identifies a confusion in the argument between what he calls *epistemic relativity* ('which asserts that all beliefs are socially produced, so that all knowledge is transient, and neither truth values nor criteria of rationality exist out of historical time', p. 57), and *judgemental relativism* (which asserts that 'all beliefs (statements) are equally valid', p. 57). Bhaskar rejects the latter as false but argues that the thesis of epistemic relativity is correct. The grounds of Bhaskar's argument stress the conceptual foundations of rational knowledge.

Once the conceptual foundations of knowledge have been accepted, there is an educational challenge to establish dialogue between different perspectives, whether they arise from competing scientific theories, different religious and ethical codes, or conflicting cultural practices. Such conflicts are constantly present in society. For example, how will the different perceptions of women and their roles in the church be resolved by the Roman Catholic Church and the Church of England? How and why has the British Royal Court adapted its tradition of 'arranged' marriages? Any educational system which permits the discussion and evaluation of differing perspectives will come up against the difficulty of resolving the conflicts between different cultures and practices. There will be a number of complex philosophical problems en route. Nevertheless, there is no educational merit in the pretence of straightforward objectivity and rationality, nor in the rejection of the values and potential of cultural diversity and its educational consequences. Moreover, there are good reasons to question those 'anti-multiculturalist' stances which include an elitism that unquestioningly affirms the values of 'high culture' and its conception of 'objectivity' and 'standards'.

Multiculturalism and anti-racism: poles apart?

The conflict between multicultural and anti-racist approaches has been fought across different kinds of terrain. There are no symptoms of relativism in the anti-racist approach, which has challenged multicultural education for serious omissions. The Institute of Race Relations statement to the Committee of Inquiry into the education of children from ethnic minority groups is a source of a characteristically direct expression of the argument.

The Institute of Race Relations statement to the Rampton Committee (IRR, 1980) was published with the title 'Anti-racist not multicultural education'. The Institute's brief submission expressed misgivings about the way in which the educational problem was posed by the brief of the committee, given that it referred exclusively to the educational needs and attainments of children from ethnic minority groups.

The Institute argued against the implications of such an approach:

> We feel . . . that an ethnic or cultural approach to the educational needs and attainments of racial minorities evades the fundamental reasons for their disabilities – which are the racialist attitudes and the racist practices in the larger society and in the educational system itself. (IRR, 1980, p. 82)

The differential weighting given to particular differences within a racial hierarchy, rather than any distinguishing characteristics of the ethnic minorities, are at the root of the problem. In this context multiculturalism

> leaves unaltered the racist fabric of the educational system. And education itself comes to be seen in terms of an adjustment process within a racialist society and not as a force for changing the values that make society racialist. (IRR, 1980, p. 82)

51

There is an essential component missing from multicultural education: learning about the racism of the dominant culture:

> Just to learn about other people's cultures . . . is not to learn about the racism of one's own. To learn about the racism of one's own culture, on the other hand, is to approach cultures objectively. (IRR, 1980, p. 82)

Anti-racist education is presented as a perspective which subsumes education about other cultures. Its implications for teacher education are that racialist attitudes and racist practices in the educational system would be reviewed. This would include systematic overhaul of methods of teaching, materials, administrative routines, and the organization and content of the curriculum and syllabus. The concerns which would then be addressed are:

> the institutional racism within the educational system as a whole in which large numbers of minority children are consigned to ESN and 'sink' schools, and streamed out of exam-entry classes, or directed away from 'academic' subjects to craft and manual subjects. (IRR, 1980, p. 82)

Does multiculturalism subsume anti-racism?

Parekh (1986) summarizes and responds to this and related criticism of multicultural education (e.g., Gurnah, 1984). He extracts four major elements of the anti-racist critique of multicultural education. These are, first, the objective of removing racism (and the argument that multicultural education is inadequate for this task), for which anti-racist education is needed. Second, the argument that multicultural education strengthens racism, serving as a kind of tranquillizer for the black community which offers positive self-images to young black people and makes white people more tolerant. Third, that multicultural education diverts black resistance into harmless channels (through work in 'the race relations industry' and by co-option), thus pacifying ethnic minorities. Finally, there is the argument that by viewing racism as an attitudinal phenomenon, the structural roots of racism are ignored and the underlying processes of exploitation of blacks by whites and its ideological rationalization will continue.

Parekh argues that these criticisms are not persuasive. He suggests that 'the so-called anti-racist education is likely to be either not education at all but anti-racist propaganda, or is in substance little different from multicultural education' (Parekh, 1986, p. 30). He suggests that the recommendations for the curriculum which come from the advocates of anti-racism are very similar to multiculturalism, and that the impact of the curriculum and the ethos of the school upon pupils is substantial. The role of the school as an educational institution which challenges racism through the enforcement of school rules and fosters understanding through the curriculum is essential to Parekh's argument:

> In these and other ways the school can hope to undercut the intellectual and moral roots of racism and weaken it. It cannot, of course, hope to eliminate it altogether, for education has its limits and the social and political roots of racism lie beyond the control of the school. However, it can make its distinctive contribution by tackling the intellectual and moral basis of racism that is amenable to and indeed falls within its purview. To ask it to do more is perhaps the surest way to ensure that it will not be able to do even this much. (Parekh, 1986, p. 31)

Synthesizing multiculturalism and anti-racism: are they two sides of the same coin?

Some authors represent multicultural education and anti-racism as perspectives which are incapable of reconciliation (e.g., Troyna, 1987). Despite arguing that the two perspectives contain a series of antagonisms, Grinter seeks a reconciliation. He argues that:

> Multicultural and antiracist education are essential to each other. They are logically connected and each alone is inadequate. Each

is appropriate to different stages and contexts in education and must be part of a combined strategy if either is to have any real effect. (Grinter, 1985, p. 7)

The synthesis, which Grinter labels *anti-racist multiculturalism*, is a gradualist approach with the following components: it incorporates a diversity of cultural references through the curriculum; it raises questions about justice and equality; it has a methodology which helps to provide skills for black pupils (and offers support and sympathy in the struggle for justice); it relates to wider issues than race (especially gender and class). Grinter emphasizes that 'Education for equality is the essential context for an anti-racist multiculturalism' (p. 8). The academic requirements of the approach are also stressed:

> Anti-racist multicultural teaching must have academic credibility, by providing as good if not a better education in basic skills and understanding through academic subjects as the existing ethnocentric treatment. (Grinter, 1985, p. 9)

The arguments surrounding the multicultural anti-racist education distinction have covered considerable ground. They have focused upon a number of contested areas, ranging from conceptions of society through the purposes of education, to aspects of school ethos and the details of the curriculum. Have the arguments been worth it? At best they have clarified part of the conceptual basis of education and led on to consideration of good educational practice. To the extent that the debate has become self-perpetuating, inward-looking and fundamentally resting upon a series of polarizations, it has been less useful. Schools are complex institutions; changes in their routine practices require appropriately complex considerations of strategies. Change in schools requires the negotiation of individual and collective action together with careful analysis of procedures and routines. Any approach which does not synthesize an understanding of the interaction of goals and purposes with structures will be inadequate. Consequently, the reservations of Craft and Klein about the arguments and their relevance to practice in schools are appropriate:

> The polarisation in the current literature, of 'multiculturalists' as simply concerned with diversity, and 'anti-racists' as concerned with the struggle for equality, is not helpful to practice in schools; these are *not* polar opposites; they share a complex interrelation-ship ... The 'multicultural' and 'antiracist' approaches are ... not *alternatives*, but interlocking parts of one whole; each is essential, but neither is sufficient on its own. (Craft and Klein, 1986)

The educational debates have grown out of interpretations of educational practice, and educational practice has, in turn, been affected by the educational debates. The changes in educational policy at the level of central government, which we now consider, bring us closer to educational practice.

Central government policies from immigrant education to education for all

Piecemeal local authority responses to the changing composition of schools, including the establishment of language centres and 'bussing', preceded central government direction in the 1960s. However, by the 1980s the policies and structures established by central government were instrumental in propelling some local authorities towards multicultural education, or at least providing sources of legitimation for those working for change from within local authorities.

Central government policy developments

The trends of central government policy, from concerns about the assimilation of immigrant pupils through discussion of integration to multiculturalism, are apparent from a number of directives, investigations, reports and statements in Parliament. The concern with the assimilation of immigrant pupils is apparent in Circular 7/65 (*The Education of Immigrants*) from the Department of Education and Science, which identifies the major educational task as the teaching of English, identifies ethnic minority pupils as an educational problem, and shows anxieties about the responses of white parents to the concentration of immigrant children in schools. Investigations at about that time included a collection of statistics on 'immigrant' children, begun in 1966. Funding for specific initiatives by local authorities with a substantial number of ethnic minority people was provided under Section 11 of the Local Government Act 1966.

The moves towards integration are less clear-cut, but were apparent in in-service courses and some official publications. Later, as evidence accumulated, particularly from the West Indian community, educational sources, and the Select Committee on Race Relations, about the educational achievements of ethnic minority pupils, the limitations of these early perspectives began to be acknowledged.

The Swann Report

In 1977 the Select Committee on Race Relations and Immigration reported on the West Indian community, and urgently recommended an inquiry into the causes of educational underachievement of children of West Indian origin and action to improve the situation. Subsequently, in 1979, the Government set up a committee to enquire into the education of children from all ethnic minority groups. The focus was to be upon the educational performance of ethnic minority pupils and there was a requirement

> to give early and particular attention to the educational needs and attainments of pupils of West Indian origin and to make interim recommendations as soon as possible on action which might be taken in the interests of this group. (DES, 1985, p. vii)

However, this was preceded by a qualification which set the overall frame of reference of the final report:

Recognising the contribution of schools in preparing all pupils for life in a society which is both multi-racial and culturally diverse, the Committee is required to ... (DES, 1985, p. vii)

The interim findings were published in 1981 under the title *West Indian Children in Our Schools* and the final report, *Education for All*, was published in 1985. The original chair-person of the committee (Rampton) was replaced in May 1981 by Lord Swann. There were also a number of resignations from the committee.

The final report rejected the approaches of the 1960s and the 1970s:

we regard both the assimilationist and integrationist educational responses to the needs of ethnic minority pupils as, in retrospect, misguided and ill-founded. (DES, 1985, p. 198)

The committee favoured an approach which would lead towards pluralism, with the development of distinctive ethnic minority communities occurring under a framework of com-monly accepted values. The main points of the committee's argument were summarized as follows:

(a) The fundamental change that is necessary is the recognition that the problem facing the education system is not how to educate children of ethnic minorities but how to educate *all* children.

(b) Britain is a multi-racial and multi-cultural society and all pupils must be enabled to understand what this means.

(c) This challenge cannot be left to the separate and independent initiatives of LEAs and schools: only those with experience of substantial numbers of ethnic minority pupils have attempted to tackle it, though the issue affects all schools and all pupils.

(d) Education has to be something more than the reinforcement of the beliefs, values and identity which each child brings to school.

(e) It is necessary to combat racism, to attack inherited myths and stereotypes, and the ways in which they are embodied in institutional practices.

(f) Multi-cultural understanding has also to permeate all aspects

57

of a school's work. It is not a separate topic that can be welded on to existing practices.

(g) Only in this way can schools begin to offer anything approaching the *equality of opportunity* for all pupils which it must be the aspiration of the education system to provide. (DES, 1985, p. 769)

One section of the report considered the issue of racism, with an emphasis upon racism defined in attitudinal terms:

> We believe that racism is an insidious evil which, for the sake of the future unity and stability of our society, must be countered ... We believe that for schools to allow racist attitudes to persist unchecked in fact constitutes a fundamental mis-education for their pupils. (DES, 1985, p. 36)

The report was wide-ranging in its discussion. It exceeded 800 pages, and included technical papers and other contributions by individuals and groups in appendices to the chapters. In addition to the 'education for all' argument, with its historical prologue and discussion of racism, the main sections of the report covered aspects of educational achievement and under-achievement, issues of language and language education, religion and the role of the school (including reference to debates about separate schools for ethnic minorities), teacher education (including the employment of ethnic minority teachers) and a series of essays on 'other' ethnic minority groups (Chinese, Cypriot, Italian, Ukrainian, Vietnamese, 'Liverpool blacks', travellers' children, etc.). Material in the appendices included summaries of research, local education authority and school policies, curriculum outlines, statistical data, and language activities for pupils.

The report reflected the constructions of the original objectives, the diversity of the large committee (with its changing membership), and the ambiguities of the political context of the time. These separate elements contributed to the nature of the report as a kind of loosely packaged compendium of discussion, evidence, policies and recommendations. Responses to the report reflected different ways of reading it. If read as a theoretical document about, say, racism and education, its attention to institutional or structural features and the relationship between class and education appears inadequate. If some sections are read as an analysis of ethnic minorities and educational achievement, then the categorization of pupils as 'West Indian' or 'Asian' is too general to contribute much to explanation. However, more positively, there are many examples of educational practice and policy which can be used as a basis for discussion or models for development in schools. There is research evidence of the complexities of interaction between teachers and pupils in the classroom which can be used to link with the analysis of classroom practice.

The report does not provide a blueprint or template which could be used as a model for schools or teacher education. However, it does contain a great deal which can be used in discussion and in the development of guidelines for action.

Recommendations from Swann and their implementation

The report was commissioned during one political party's rule (Labour) and completed well into the lifetime of the administration of another (Conservative). Its Foreword, written by the Secretary of State for Education and Science (Sir Keith Joseph), reveals the cool response from the government, and signals one of the emerging directions of educational policy:

> The Government is firmly committed to the principle that all children, irrespective of race, colour or ethnic origin, should have a good education which develops their abilities and aptitudes to the full and brings about a true sense of belonging to Britain.

The administrative processes of the implementation of 'education for all' contained in the recommendations included reference to HM Inspectorate, local education authorities and schools, the School Curriculum Development Committee, and examining boards. The committee recommended that local education authorities should make declarations of commitment

59

to 'the principles of "education for all", to the development of a pluralist approach to the curriculum, and to countering the influence of racism' (p. 770). They recommended the appointment of senior staff in local education authorities to promote policy. They recommended that *all* schools should review their work in the light of the principles of 'education for all', and adopt policies to deal with racism.

These levers and mechanisms for change were constructed and put in place in the following years. Their effects became clear in some GCSE subject guidelines, in the requirements of the Council for the Accreditation of Teacher Education, and in the reports of HM Inspectorate on schools and colleges. In addition, 'teaching in a multi-ethnic society' became a priority for in-service education for teachers (for two years), with funding for attendance at 25-day courses as a means of promoting policy implementation. These aspects of the implementation of the report provided opportunities which were taken with varying degrees of enthusiasm and commitment by local education authorities, head-teachers, and teachers.

Local authority policy developments

As mentioned above, there were piecemeal responses from local authorities in the late 1950s and 1960s to the settlement of ethnic minorities. These included separate educational provision for some pupils in language centres before their integration into schools, daily transportation of black pupils to ensure their dispersal, and the use of extra staff in some schools gained through Section 11 funding.

Eventually, most local authorities developed systematic policies on education for a multicultural society. Whereas the first moves were made by those with established black communities, a number of predominantly white local authorities were relatively quick to respond to the emerging concerns of the 1980s. These local education authority policies reflected particular phases of the development of educational ideologies (and included some anachronistic drafts). Some also show evidence of responses to the specific populations of the areas covered and the groups with which the local authority has to negotiate. For example, Calderdale's policy acknowledges the large proportion of Muslims amongst its Asian population. Meanwhile, Hampshire's major policy document is topped and tailed by classical quotations from the ancient Greeks and Edmund Burke, appropriate to the sensibilities of its conservative political composition.

The content of local education authority policy statements and their processes of design and implementation are important to the continued development of multicultural education. Two examples are given here, one from the early 1980s and one from the late 1980s. They are the policies of Berkshire and Hampshire.

Early 1980s anti-racism: Berkshire's policies and their development

Berkshire's policy was developed through a lengthy period of consultation and discussion which began in the late 1970s. These consultations involved people both from within the county and outside, and led to a major policy statement in three parts: a general policy, an outline of its implications, and a programme for support.

In notes for a talk (given to members of the Voluntary Colleges Working Party on Multicultural Education), Robin Richardson (at that time Multicultural Advisor for Berkshire) identifies three misunderstandings about policy documents:

> Policy documents are not *from* certain people *to* certain people, but are the expressions of a process of negotiation – that is, bargaining and arguing – between and amongst largely autonomous groupings ...
>
> Policy documents are not definitive statements, but are tentative crystallisations of consensus and of dispute at one particular point in time ...
>
> LEAs are not adequately pictured as hierarchies or pyramids,

each with a top (the Education Committee, the CEO, and his staff), a middle (headteachers) and a bottom (classrooms). This mental model of LEAs as hierarchies hugely overestimates the influence of people 'at the top', of them; and hugely underestimates the power of people 'at the bottom' to resist influence from others, and to exert influence themselves. Further, it hugely underestimates the actual and potential influence of parents, communities and pressure groups.

The time-scale for the development of a formal policy by Berkshire was about four years. In 1979–1980 two education sub-committees (Reading Council for Racial Equality and Slough Council for Community Relations) made recommendations about a formal policy statement. An ad hoc working group was formed in 1981 followed by the establishment, in the autumn by the Education Committee, of an Advisory Committee for Multicultural Education. This advisory committee, with about 40 members representing a wide range of groups and with two external consultants, prepared and circulated a discussion paper, and subsequently a final report including a policy statement, in December 1982. The education committee approved an amended form of the policy statement in January 1983. This was followed by widespread consultation with schools and community organizations and in the autumn of 1983 a budget and time-scale for the implementation of the policy were approved by the education committee. The policy documents, when circulated, requested responses to the director by three dates, of which the last was 31 March 1984.

The formal statement at the beginning of Berkshire's general policy paper is as follows:

Berkshire County Council requires and supports all its educational institutions and services to create, maintain and promote racial equality and justice.

The Council is opposed to racism in all its forms. It wishes therefore:

1) To promote understanding of the principles and practices of racial equality and justice, and commitment to them.
2) To identify and remove all practices, procedures and customs which discriminate against ethnic minority people and to replace them with procedures which are fair to all.
3) To encourage ethnic minority parents and communities to be fully involved in the decision-making processes which affect the education of their children.
4) To increase the influence of ethnic minority parents, organisations and communities by supporting educational and cultural projects which they themselves initiate.
5) To encourage the recruitment of ethnic minority teachers, administrators and other staff at all levels, and the appointment of ethnic minority governors.
6) To monitor and evaluate the implementation of County Council policies, and to make changes and corrections as appropriate.
(Royal County of Berkshire, 1983)

The remainder of this policy paper provided clarification of the concerns with equality and justice, and an analysis of aspects of racism. The second and third policy papers outlined the major implications for schools and the ways in which the policy would be practically implemented.

Late 1980s synthesis: Hampshire's policy

Hampshire is not a county with a large proportion of ethnic minority people; it falls some way below the national average, with 2.0 per cent registered as having been born in the New Commonwealth and Pakistan according to the 1981 census. Southampton has 3.0 per cent – a total of 6,020 – while Portsmouth has 2.3 per cent – a total of 4,022 people. Hampshire's policy is a demonstration of the way in which a predominantly white area has attempted to respond to the educational needs of a multicultural society. It also reveals some of the gains made through the experiences of earlier policy development by other local education authorities.

The Hampshire Education Committee approved a policy in June 1986. Its general policy reads as follows:

The Hampshire Education Service should prepare pupils and students for life in a multicultural society by developing an ethos and a curriculum which:

(a) reflect and value cultural diversity and turn it to advantage in enriching pupils' and students' experience and understanding of the world in which they live;

(b) recognise and counter racial prejudice;

(c) foster racial harmony and understanding amongst all in society; and

(d) offer all pupils and students equality of opportunity and an education for life in a culturally and racially plural society.

This policy should permeate the whole curriculum and find expression in all aspects of school and college life. (Hampshire County Council Education Department, 1988)

The themes of cultural diversity and pluralism are emphasized in a statement in the introduction to Hampshire's policy:

In a culturally diverse society such as ours, education which reflects and celebrates this diversity is simply good education. (p. 6)

The need to challenge racism, if this pluralism is to be achieved, is recognized and stated as follows, drawing attention to the relative invisibility of it in the county:

This vision of a truly pluralist society in which diversity is recognised and celebrated – as part of an interdependent world – is most threatened by the fact of racism. In an area like Hampshire it is easy to be blind to this reality for so much of it lies below the surface, and is subtly part of our everyday assumptions and *taken for granted* view of the world. Widespread and persistent racial harassment such as racial abuse, graffiti and violence, are but surface indicators of those deeper sets of attitudes and practices which challenge our traditional claim to uphold civilised values. (p. 6)

The policy shows recognition of opposition to multicultural education, makes reference to some of the stereotyping of those actively involved in the policy process, and emphasizes the need to state educational goals positively:

Let us recognise an irony. Multicultural education, which uses concepts such as 'prejudice', 'stereotype' and 'labelling', is itself a prime victim of these processes. The first task therefore is to create a climate in which we can all risk failure. This is after all an important part of the learning process, and we are all learners. To approach the task in an over-earnest and zealous way will, by creating anxiety, only block change. Multicultural education is not the preserve of the ideologically pure. We must develop skills in others, not disable them. That is why it is better to stress what we are for in education, not simply what we are against. (p. 7)

Multicultural education is recognized as part of a process which is constantly changing but which (hopefully) will not be reversed:

It ought to be apparent then that one can never *do* multicultural education, either in a subject sense or as part of a checklist that has been ticked off and completed. It is a task that, once started, can never be finished, for each generation presents a fresh challenge. What we can do is to so develop within the service the thinking, values and practices which lie at the heart of multicultural education, that we can at least dispense with the label, and simply talk about good education for all and enhance our delivery of it. (p. 8)

The Hampshire document was designed to be a practical resource for teachers with information (including a summary of key points of the Swann Report), guidelines and practical exercises for teachers. It is a document designed to assist the process of review and negotiation of new policies.

The effects of permeation of the curriculum by a multicultural dimension are intended to be progressive through any pupil's educational career. The task of developing continuity and increased understanding of other cultures, together with the normal social and intellectual development of children and young people, is complex. It requires, if it is to be successfully accomplished, co-ordination across a range of subject areas within schools. It also demands communication and co-operation between schools at different levels of education. This aspect of multiculturalism makes it as clear as any other that it is not just a task for one teacher in a classroom in isolation, nor even for all the teachers at one school. If it is to be successfully accomplished it requires a systematic network of discussion, consultation and negotiation.

Hampshire's outline of continuity in multicultural education through the curriculum covers the full range of education from infant to post-16. It incorporates many of the diverse strands of multiculturalism, together with the concern with racism which emerged in the debates of the early 1980s. It requires innovations in the curriculum, support from school rules and procedures, and links between the school and community.

A Strategy Grid for Continuity in Multicultural Education

Phase	Inputs	Outcomes
Infant	1. Affirmation – valuing everyone	1. Positive self-image
	2. Teaching through mother tongue/dialect where appropriate	2. Language awareness/multilingualism
	3. Using non-ethnocentric learning resources – books, artefacts	3. Positive attitude towards cultural diversity within the school and community
	4. Experiencing other cultures – indirectly and directly through visits, visitors and learning resources	4. Awareness and understanding of change
Junior	5. Exploring distant communities in topic work – national and global studies which are small scale and concrete	5. Awareness of bias and stereotyping in relation to cultural groups
	6. Exploring bias in books, pictures, TV, etc	6. Perspective consciousness – political literacy

Phase	Inputs	Outcomes
Secondary and post-16	7. Exploring value systems and events worldwide: how individuals and groups view the world differently and the interrelatedness of world events	7. Sympathetic understanding of others
	8. Exploring the nature of prejudice and racism – in individual, group and societal terms. Historical and contemporary examples of racism	8. A global sense of identification and interdependence: local national and international citizenship

Other sources of policy

The education system is never isolated from the other institutions of society. In the mid-1980s people at all levels of education were involved in the redesign of education to take into account the ideas and examples of good practice in multicultural and anti-racist education. Policies reflecting their particular orientations, sources of legitimation, and spheres of influence were produced by churches both nationally and locally (e.g., the Roman Catholic Church (1985)); different levels of higher education concerned with teacher education (e.g., the CNAA; the Voluntary Colleges Working Party on Multicultural Education); and trade unions (e.g., the National Association of Head Teachers; the National Union of Teachers; the Assistant Masters and Mistresses Association). In different ways, and with varying degrees of pressure, these policies influenced the processes of institutional change.

As general and pervasive as these policies may seem and as authoritative as they are, with direction from central and local government, it would be mistaken to assume that they were ever uniformly adopted. Some of the phases described in policy documents occurred more on paper and in discussion (perhaps especially the 'integrationist' phase) than in practice.

67

There was considerable trepidation amongst those attempting change in the early and mid-1980s. For example, there were rumours of a headteacher trying to develop school practice without external publicity in order to avoid exposure to unreasoned criticism from governors and parents. There were allegations that a local authority adviser in an 'all-white' county was asked not to publicize the responsibility for multicultural education which was given in addition to the role of special needs adviser.

At the level of the school, there has been considerable variation in the spirit and form of the implementation of central or local government policy. Moreover, there are structures within education which have worked against the development of education for a multicultural society. Thus, in the late 1980s, there remained schools with most of the hallmarks of the assimilationist 1960s in their approach to the curriculum and in their procedures and policies. There are even schools where headteachers' interpretation of their specific task of providing education linked with a particular form of Christianity has had the effect of maintaining a degree of ethnic exclusiveness or segregation. This process has been aided by the particular preferences of some white parents.

In some ways, the changes and developments which have occurred are radical and have led to profound modifications of policy and practice in schools. Although they have been identified by some as part of the package of social control (Gurnah, 1984), others have viewed them as providing equality of opportunity rather than unfair discrimination. At the root of these concerns there has been a quest to provide a good education for all pupils. There has also been recognition that all of the potential gains of these general or global policy orientations could be lost in a classroom where dull, rather than imaginative, teaching occurred, or in a school where a repressive rather than a facilitative regime pertained. The developments within schools are the next issue for consideration.

Developments within schools

Implications for the curriculum

It is in schools that the transformations are made which link educational ideologies and policies with everyday practice. To illustrate some of the effects of multicultural education upon schools, two core areas of the curriculum – mathematics and language – will be considered (other aspects of school practice will be raised in Chapter 3). The first example, mathematics, relates to the education of all pupils, whether in predominantly white or multi-ethnic schools. It demonstrates the way in which the implementation of the principles derived from multi-cultural/anti-racist education can lead to an enhancement of the mathematical skills of pupils, and a better understanding of the development and application of mathematical knowledge. The second example, concerned with language and bilingualism, is one which focuses upon the educational needs of some ethnic minority pupils. Here, it is possible to see the interaction of ideologies, educational research evidence and policy in a different way, with the political context of education shaping the implementation of policy and arguably constraining the possibilities of education.

The Swann Report argued that the curriculum in all schools should be permeated by themes which would develop children's and young people's understanding of the contributions to knowledge made by other cultures. This recommendation was considered appropriate to all subject areas. Criteria for evaluation of the curriculum from the Schools Council which were suggested in evidence to the Swann committee, and were reproduced in the report with approval, demonstrate this objective and show some of the additional concerns about the effects of the curriculum:

  i. The variety of social, cultural and ethnic groups and a perspective of the world should be evident in visuals, stories, conversation and information.

ii. People from social, cultural and ethnic groups should be presented as individuals with every human attribute.
iii. Cultures should be empathetically described in their own terms and not judged against some notion of 'ethnocentric' or 'Eurocentric' culture.
iv. The curriculum should include accurate information on racial and cultural differences and similarities.

In addition to expressing their strong support for the above, the Swann committee listed two more criteria:

All children should be encouraged to see the cultural diversity of our society in a positive light.
The issue of racism, at both institutional and individual level, should be considered openly and efforts made to counter it. (DES, 1985, pp. 328–9)

The curriculum as a whole might cover these six objectives but of course no single subject in isolation is likely to cover all of them. There are opportunities for contributions from every subject within the curriculum (Craft and Bardell, 1984; Arora and Duncan, 1986). Each subject area, from art to personal and social education, is taught through references to distinctive cultural themes or artefacts. This is particularly clear in the case of mathematics teaching.

Mathematics
Mathematics is a subject which carries cultural messages in a teaching context through its content and methods of teaching. In maths lessons in the 1950s, problems involving the calculation of compound interest on building society accounts; the profit margins made by small shopkeepers from buying and selling tea; the gains from the purchase and sale of stocks and shares at different prices; the probabilities of drawing certain cards from a pack of playing cards; the likelihood of winning the pools; and the best design for a can of baked beans to maximize volume and minimize the metal used in its construction, provided pupils with everyday knowledge which would

be relevant to their lives. Historical anecdotes about Pythagoras, Pascal, and other contributors to the development of mathematical ideas and solutions established the cultural background of the progress, achievements, and mathematical sophistication of European culture.

End-of-term amusements with mathematical puzzles may have provided incidental reinforcement of Eurocentric world views. An example is the problem of the querulous man on holiday on a South Seas island with two tribes, one of whose members always tell the truth, and the other whose members always tell lies: how does he know which question to ask to find the way to the next village? (Gardner, 1959).

In the 1980s, teachers began to use examples of mathematical development from a range of cultural sources as a means of extending and reinforcing the mathematical skills and understanding of pupils. These have included opportunities to use exercises and demonstrations in counting (one system of finger counting, of Chinese origin, allows representation of any number up to 100,000 on the five fingers of one hand); geometry (employing patterns, designs and shapes from Hindu, Sikh and Muslim sources); and statistics (using data on, for example, languages or religious backgrounds) (Hemmings, 1984).

References to the history of mathematics, which have been used by teachers to illustrate and explain mathematical points and the everyday uses of mathematical ideas, have drawn on examples from India (use of numerical symbols), China (the equivalent of what is commonly referred to as Pascal's triangle, some 300 years before Pascal's birth; solutions of simultaneous equations some 500 years before European equivalents), and Islamic civilization.

In addition to providing a more accurate understanding of the development of mathematics than a Eurocentric interpretation, these methods of teaching incorporate valuable ways of constructive repetition which can enhance the interest and understanding of pupils.

71

Language and bilingualism

It has been estimated that more than half of the world's population is bilingual. In countries which do not have bilingual traditions, those who are not accomplished in the dominant language, but are bilingual or developing bilinguals, may be judged to be suffering from a considerable cognitive deficit which can best be remedied by educational programmes involving attention to the dominant language only. In addition to resting upon certain educational assumptions, such an approach is based upon social and cultural considerations about the values of bilingualism and the cultural forms associated with other languages.

In the 1950s and 1960s, as mentioned above, educational programmes for 'immigrant' pupils whose first language was not English were concentrated upon instruction in English and education was conducted entirely through English. A central component of the understanding of the situation at the time has recently been termed 'the myth of the bilingual handicap' (Cummins, 1981, 1984; Hamers and Blanc, 1989). It was assumed that bilingualism itself was an educational handicap and that the solution was to teach the dominant language and to use it for education. The major features of the educational assumptions about this assimilationist approach are outlined by Cummins in a model which is based upon educational approaches in the United States in the 1920s but which also applies to other countries.

The myth of the bilingual handicap

A.
Overt aim
Teach English to minority children in order to create a harmonious society with equal opportunity for all.

Covert aim
Anglicize minority children because linguistic and cultural diversity are seen as a threat to social cohesion.

B.
Method
Prohibit use of first language (L1) in schools and make children reject their own culture and language in order to identify with majority English group.

Justification
1. L1 should be eradicated because it will interfere with the learning of English.
2. Identification with L1 culture will reduce child's ability to identify with English-speaking culture.

C.
Results
1. Shame in L1 language and culture.
2. Replacement of L1 by second language (L2).
3. School failure among many children.

'Scientific' explanation
1. Bilingualism causes confusion in thinking, emotional insecurity, and school failures.
2. Minority group children are 'culturally deprived' by definition since they are not Anglos.
3. Some minority language groups are genetically inferior (common theory in the United States in the 1920s and 1930s).

Outcomes
Even more intense efforts by the school to eradicate the deficiencies inherent in minority children.

The failure of these efforts only serves to reinforce the myth of minority group deficiencies. (adapted from Cummins, 1981)

The Swann Report argued in favour of fostering the linguistic identities of ethnic minority communities, recognizing that linguistic diversity in Britain is a positive feature of contemporary society. It recommended that school premises be made available for community use for the development of ethnic minority languages. It did not support the implementation of bilingual programmes of education in school. Rather, a supporting role could be provided for non-English-speaking children by a 'bilingual resource' who would assist a teacher during a period of transition, especially in nursery classes.

In a review of work on language and bilingualism, Hamers and Blanc (1989) offer a trenchant critique of these conclusions:

> In the United Kingdom, an 800-page government report (*Education for All*, 1985, known as the 'Swann Report') completely misinterpreted research data on mother-tongue teaching and bilingual education and concluded that education should provide better ESL programs, but that mother-tongue education should be the responsibility of ethnolinguistic minorities. These conclusions, both in the United States and the United Kingdom, were reached on exclusively ideological grounds: they completely disregard the existing empirical evidence on bilingual education, and in particular the consequences for minority children of teaching exclusively through the mainstream language. (Hamers and Blanc, 1989, p. 192)

Use of a language other than the mother-tongue for teaching is seen as a 'subtractive' situation, since it is part of a process of replacing or subtracting the pupil's first language, which devalues that language and the accompanying culture. On the other hand, use of the mother-tongue for teaching can be seen as 'additive', since it positively values the child's mother tongue and culture, leads to cognitive enhancement, and increases power in the development of language skills (Hamers and Blanc, 1989).

There now exists a substantial amount of research which supports the enhanced educational, cognitive, and social consequences of mother-tongue teaching. The implications of such work are that positive evaluation of the mother tongue educationally, and its appropriate use in education, lead to patterns of educational achievement where bilinguals are superior to monolinguals in a number of tasks:

From the conception of the bilingual as someone whose speech shows interferences and who is at worst cognitively deficient and at best the sum of two monolinguals, we have moved to the conception of an integrated person, 'a unique and specific speaker-hearer, a communicator of a different sort' . . . for whom bilingual experience may enhance cognitive functioning. (Hamers and Blanc, 1989, p. 257)

Acceptance of this interpretation of the research evidence on bilingualism in schools would have implications for language learning generally and not just for ethnic minority pupils who are developing bilinguals.

Conclusions

This chapter has considered four general questions: (i) what are the major approaches to education in a multicultural society? (ii) what policies have been followed by central government? (iii) what policies have been developed by local education authorities? (iv) what are the implications of this for the school curriculum?

In dealing with each question, the arguments and controversies have been briefly outlined. The trends in central and local government policy have also been summarized. The continuing process of the debates about bilingual education and the lack of consensus is made particularly clear in the final discussion. Chapter 3 examines the issue of racism, which is central to the evaluation of policy and which has implications for the school curriculum and school practices.

3 The challenge of racism: response and counter-response

Whereas assimilationist educational responses are based upon the assumption that ethnic minority pupils are a problem, many educational policy-makers in the 1980s have faced the possibility that there is something about the white majority which is a problem. The reversal of the equation is typified by the challenging comment, 'Black people are not a problem; black people have problems; white people are the problem'. The issue at the core of this challenge is racism. It is this issue which, implicitly or explicitly, appears at the centre of the conflicts about the direction of education for a multicultural society.

This chapter examines the issue of racism in society and in schools. It is organized around six general questions. The first two are mainly concerned with conceptual issues. They are: What is 'race'? and What is racism? The next two are concerned with the elucidation of social processes: How does racism operate in society? and How does racism operate in schools? The fifth question is concerned with the responses of schools: What can schools do in their procedures and in their teaching to deal with racism? The final question is a kind of check: How are the issues to be raised?

'Race'

Contemporary fixations on differences between groups in British society might suggest some continuity about racial differences and a sense of permanence about how different people

76

are categorized. However, a historical overview of the development of popular and 'scientific' thought on race reveals that there have been marked shifts in the basis of categorization of people, and that different forms of typification have been used (Banton, 1987). As a European example, the Celts have been identified as people sharing similar qualities on the basis of culture, language, territory and social organization, with each application yielding different boundaries (Baker, 1974). In the interests of categorizing differences between people on a worldwide basis, scientists and anthropologists have measured height; calibrated bumps on skull exteriors; assessed brain volumes by pouring lead shot into cavities within skulls; sketched nostrils; photographed breasts, buttocks and genitalia; and generally investigated the anatomies of their subjects. The category systems which have resulted from these investigations have offered as few as three and as many as thirty 'races' (Cavalli-Sforza and Feldman, 1981).

Exercises in classification require the identification and evaluation of difference. The practice of identifying and evaluating the difference is guided by a network of assumptions and general propositions. Attempts by scholars since the eighteenth century to identify human 'races' or subspecies have revealed a great deal about the working assumptions of Europeans as to their own cultural superiority and the inferiority of others (Banton, 1987).

Beneath the surface arbitrariness of these attempts at classification there lies an important issue of the recognition of variation which relates to a marked change in the development of scientific thought about evolution. Once the significance of variation is accepted, it is possible to recognize that an emphasis upon differences between groups may direct attention away from differences within those groups. Moreover, in terms of the total range of variation, any difference between groups may be insignificant. This issue and some of its consequences are made clear by Futuyma:

> To dismiss variation as unimportant and to classify specimens into discrete categories, is a manifestation of essentialism . . . It is the kind of thinking that dichotomises: either/or, black/white, good/ evil, normal/abnormal . . . the replacement of typological thinking by the recognition of variation was pivotal in the development of the modern view of evolution. (Futuyma, 1986, p. 108)

Futuyma argues that the variations amongst human populations are so great that there is no clear limit to the number of subspecies that could be recognized. Arguing from genetic evidence, Futuyma writes:

> . . . almost every human population differs from every other . . . the genetic diversity within a single 'race' is much greater than the genetic differences among 'races'; in fact, the differences among races account for only about 15% of the genetic diversity in the entire human species. (Futuyma, 1986, pp. 108–9)

Recognition of the existence of many bases of variation makes it possible to understand that the use of different criteria for classification will yield very different distributions of people across the globe. For example, the once common classification of people into three groups – Caucasoid, Negroid and Mongoloid – based upon surface considerations such as skin colour and hair type, yields a particular distribution across the major continents. Meanwhile, a classification based upon blood groups provides a considerably dissimilar grouping (Harris, 1975; Futuyma, 1986).

Models of genetic similarity and diversity make it clear that the degree of difference between human populations is slight. This point is emphasized above with reference to variation within human populations. Put another way, the genetic variation within specific human groups is almost as great as the variation amongst the total population. For example, Lewontin *et al.* (1984) argue that 'If everyone on earth became extinct except for the Kikuyu of East Africa, about 85 per cent of all human variability would still be present in the reconstituted species' (cited by Futuyma, 1986, p. 522). Such genetic differences as do exist between human groups are considered to be not only small, but considerably smaller than those which are commonly found between subspecies of other animals (Nei and Roychoudhury, 1982).

By way of conclusion, Futuyma's emphatic comments about the scientific inadequacy of the concept of 'race' are sufficient:

> The concept of race, masking the overwhelming genetic similarity of all peoples and the mosaic patterns of variation that do not correspond to racial divisions, is not only socially dysfunctional but is biologically indefensible as well. (Futuyma, 1986, p. 109)

People are all of the same species.

Racism: conceptual considerations

The expansion, elaboration, and eventual theoretical collapse of the category systems and explanations of race since the first recorded introduction of the term to the English language in the sixteenth century (Banton, 1987) is unremarkable at some levels. Scientific progress is normally rapid and the 'half-life' of scientific ideas is short, with new concepts and models inevitably being superseded, before long, by others. However, close scrutiny of the history of the concept of race is hardly necessary in order to recognize the interaction between socially formed concepts and the theory and practice of scientific investigation. The history of this aspect of biological and social science thus shows clear links with the history of imperialism, colonization, conquest and slavery. Ideologies derived from (and contributing to) the social relations between different groups have played a part in the selection and interpretation of evidence. Consequently, withdrawal of scientific support for distinctions between groups of people and the absence of scientific justification for corresponding practices of social discrimination may have little impact. 'Races' may not exist, but how does 'racism' continue?

Attention to the concepts subsumed under the general term

'racism' takes us into recent intellectual history. Banton identifies the late 1930s as the period of the word's first use in the English language (Banton, 1977). Despite the recentness of its invention, the term covers considerable ground in its broadest uses. It includes aspects of people's attitudes, routine behaviour, and culture (and their interconnections); social institutions and their history; issues of language, discourse, and ideology; and, finally, moral evaluation. This combination of complexity and evaluation poses particularly difficult problems for understanding racism in education, for promoting educational change and for teaching about ethnic and community relations.

Are these concepts useful? Do they shed light on what goes on in schools and the effects of education? Is it better to avoid references to prejudice and racism by use of a style of language which substitutes more general terms such as inequality and discrimination? Such questions, which challenge the value of the central and subsidiary concepts of racism, are best answered after consideration of the evidence about racism in society and in education. Since they are raised in theoretical discussion and in contexts of educational change, they can usefully be borne in mind.

Racism: some basic concepts

Racialization has been used as a general term to cover the ways in which some people have come to be defined by others in terms of assumed biological characteristics (Banton, 1977; Reeves, 1983; Miles, 1989). The processes of racialization have varied and have not solely been based upon skin colour. British reaction to the Irish, both in Ireland and after their migration to Britain, has included responses to the Irish as if they were a 'race' with particular characteristics.

The term *racism* has a complex history which includes subdivision into several types (Halstead, 1988); and, after some expansion of its use, attempts to argue for limits to its application (Miles, 1989). In educational contexts, discussion of the form and effects of racism has commonly identified three different levels of analysis. These are:

(a) individual – which is concerned with actions and attitudes involving the negative evaluation of people on the basis of some assumed biological characteristic such as skin colour;
(b) institutional – which is concerned with routine procedures and practices and the ways in which they can exclude or disadvantage people;
(c) structural – which is concerned with the broader, historically embedded patterns of social inequality in society with reference to, for example, work, housing or education.

In practice these levels are, of course, interconnected. Teachers' opinions about categories of pupils can be expressed in direct ways in interaction in the classroom (e.g., by devoting time to the control of certain types of pupils). Less directly, teachers' social assumptions about types of pupils can become part of the chain of tacit decision-making about the composition of bands and streams which can, in turn, lead to the concentration of ethnic minority pupils in lower streams. Routine gathering of information about pupils which does not accommodate the different naming systems of, say, different Asian groups, may lead to discrimination against pupils. Some pupils, as a result of a combination of circumstances including where they live, family income and housing, attend schools with buildings in poor conditions, low levels of staffing and inadequate resourcing.

The interaction of interpersonal, institutional and structural factors can be represented graphically in circular form (Figure 1). As a two-dimensional representation of processes which occur through time and which change their form, this is a simplification. However, it does have plausibility: it is possible to start from any place in the circle and work through to the other locations. For example, if people with the power to hire and fire believe that ethnic minorities or women are not capable of certain kinds of work (for example, as car mechanics

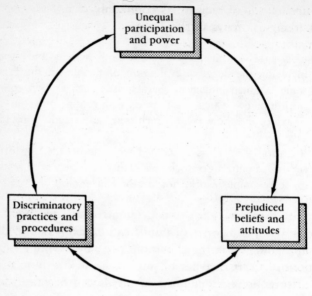

Figure 1.

or bank managers) then ethnic minorities and women are not hired as a result of discrimination in the appointment process, which may lead staff to believe that such people are incapable of such work, and so the process will continue. Similarly, if the routine for hiring people in a long-established workplace is that jobs go to 'the lads of dads', thus discriminating indirectly against ethnic minorities and women, there will be unequal participation in the workforce, which leads to certain beliefs about the capabilities and suitability of certain types of employees, and so on.

These hypothetical, simplified examples of how a process might work underestimate the complexity and subtlety of some forms of discrimination. Sets of beliefs, and procedures, can be wrapped in words, symbols, and common courtesies which conceal their negative evaluations and force. The kinds of discrimination illustrated by these examples may be invisible both to those who are discriminated against and to those who discriminate. They may be the unintended consequences of action designed for another purpose. Discussion about discriminatory action may be couched in terms which disguise their underlying racial dimensions. By contrast, the hypothetical examples above are more subtle than some forms of racism which are demonstrated intentionally and brutally through racial attacks and repetitive racial harassment.

It is through consideration of research concerned with racial discrimination in different contexts that the question of *how* racism operates can best be considered. Once the structures and mechanisms (or regular patterns of discrimination and the practices which reproduce them) are revealed, the implications for teachers and schools can be more precisely analysed.

Racism in practice – how significant is racism in Britain?

Questions of the existence and significance of racism in Britain often arise and are tackled in different ways, for with different definitions as starting points there can be varied assessments of the evidence. There are other problems, since some of the activities covered are covert, or not recognized by the people involved, and there are difficulties in assessing some of the evidence. There are also difficulties which arise from the investigation of activities known to be illegal. Nevertheless, there is an accumulation of evidence from official and unofficial sources, from surveys and experiments, which can now be drawn upon.

Reflection on the differing experiences of the majority population and ethnic minorities leads us to realize that many, if not most, acts of racism are invisible to the white majority. Some are also not clearly identifiable by those who suffer from them. Nevertheless, it is worth persisting with the examination of the processes involved. Inasmuch as Chapter 1 tends to offer a static view of society, it does not reveal the ongoing way in which divisions are recreated through the routine practices of people in key areas of life. Yet an evaluation of the presence and significance of racial discrimination depends upon the delineation of processes which operate to deny access (for example, to jobs and houses) to some people, while providing access to others. This leads to questions such as: What are the working assumptions of people in key positions and how do these link with racial discrimination? What are the institutional contexts, the institutional rules and norms which serve to discriminate against some groups? What are the outcomes of such processes?

These questions will be addressed by reference to some of the key areas of citizenship in Britain: immigration, work, housing, and safety on the streets.

Immigration policies
Policies to restrict immigration are a common feature of societies around the world. Their major purpose is normally to provide a link between economic needs and the qualities of those applying for entry. The needs to respond compassionately to those with refugee status, or with justice to those who are relatives of a country's existing citizens, are also frequently reflected – as these needs arise – in immigration policy.

A national policy to control immigration which is designed, for example, chiefly to ensure that a country allows in only those who can contribute to the economy, provide essential labour, and offer a guarantee that they possess the material and educational resources to enable them to work might involve discrimination on the basis of qualities such as identifiable skills, educational qualifications, availability of work compatible with the skills possessed, and guarantees of employment. Such a policy, which discriminated on grounds of education, skill and other personal attributes, could be implemented in ways which would not entail direct or indirect discrimination on grounds of 'race', religion, or gender. Some countries have sought to design and implement such policies.

Britain's 'gatekeeping' laws to control immigration and determine the status of people living here have included categories of entry which reflect concern to secure participation in the workforce. They also have other qualities. They have not been designed solely to ensure that immigrants have the capacity and resources to contribute to, say, the growth of the economy. The selective attention of legislation to people from the New Commonwealth and Pakistan safeguards other factors. As Dummett remarks:

> there have been many different systems of control since 1962 ... But at each stage these controls have aimed at excluding black people rather than white. (Dummett, 1986.)

However, the history of Britain's response to immigrants in ways which appear to discriminate on the basis of skin colour or culture rather than other factors goes back more than a few decades, as Table 3.1 shows.

Miles and Solomos (1987) document the discriminatory responses to seamen – in the first quarter of this century – who were British subjects (i.e. from countries within the Empire, predominantly Indian and West Indian). The tactics employed included attempts at repatriation and the use of legislation to modify their legal status so that they were covered by the Aliens Acts rather than being treated as British subjects.

Attempts to restrict Jewish migration in the late nineteenth- and early twentieth centuries followed action by Conservative MPs, trades union congresses, mass protest rallies, and political action by the 'British Brothers League'. Miles and Solomos note that 'The ideological form in which the political issue was expressed, and the motivation for some of the agitation, was explicitly racist ... and articulated with nationalism' (1987, p. 80). Subsequently, the entry of Jews fleeing from Nazi persecution was severely restricted despite some changes in policy. Miles and Solomos analyse the official rationale for the restriction of Jewish entry, and make comparisons with the numbers admitted as Dutch and Belgian citizens and under the scheme of the Polish government and citizens in exile. They argue that there was a discrepancy between public justification for policy and its implementation. Their concluding

Table 3.1 *Legislation concerning the entry and settlement of migrants to Britain*

1894	Merchant Shipping Act
1905	Aliens Order
1914	Aliens Restriction Act
1919	Aliens Restriction (Amendment) Act
1920	Aliens Order
1925	Special Restrictions (Coloured Alien Seamen) Order
1947	Polish Resettlement Act
1948	British Nationality Act
1962	Commonwealth Immigrants Act
1965	Race Relations Act
1968	Commonwealth Immigrants Act
1969	Immigration Appeals Act
1971	Immigration Act
1976	Race Relations Act
1981	British Nationality Act
1988	Immigration Act

Source: adapted from Miles and Solomos (1987).

explanation of the discrepancy is that: 'It seems more likely that the government and state officials were prepared to concede to, and thereby legitimize, the widespread racism that was evident in Britain ... and, at least in certain quarters, may even have been motivated by racism.'

The series of Immigration Acts passed in the 1960s and 1970s and the Nationality Act of the 1980s have been explicitly targeted at restricting the entry of black people from the Commonwealth. Meanwhile, the movement of people within the European Community (including Ireland) has been facilitated by a series of measures.

Official arguments supporting the restriction of black immigration have a similar structure to that used to justify the refusal of entry to Jewish people before the Second World War. At that time the Home Secretary expressed concern about the growth of an anti-Jewish movement if a significant number of Jewish refugees were admitted (Miles and Solomos, 1987). More recently, successive Home Secretaries have asserted that the key to peaceful ethnic and community relations in Britain is the refusal of entry to black people. Such arguments rest, to a significant degree, upon assumptions about the presence and mobilization of racism within the native white population. They also legitimize it and contribute to its reproduction.

The control of migration and settlement is but one aspect of the development of ideologies, structures and practices based upon discrimination. Analysis of the form and practice of immigration control and the debates about immigration clearly reveals the processes of racialization which are a part of British immigration policy. There are other features of life, which are essential to equality in citizenship, where 'gatekeeping' practices may reveal the existence of discrimination on grounds of race, culture, or religion. The next section examines two of these: work and housing.

Discriminatory processes at work

The patterns of employment and income of ethnic minorities in comparison with the majority population were discussed in Chapter 1. The general picture is one of differential employment characteristics in terms of occupation, sectors of work and income, together with higher rates of unemployment for ethnic minorities. Such differential employment may not be based upon discrimination in the workplace, or on the processes of recruitment, hiring and promotion. There are, perhaps, other factors which explain the inequalities.

Ohri and Faruqi (1988) discuss five hypotheses for the higher rates of unemployment for black people. These hypotheses are treated as single causal factors, operating in isolation, and are based upon considerations of the following:

1. The age structure of the black population;
2. the level of skills and qualifications of the black population;
3. increased discrimination by employers in hiring labour when there is a surplus of labour;
4. the regional and occupational concentrations of black workers;
5. the process of sacking those most recently hired in times of economic retrenchment.

On the basis of evidence from national and local statistics and research, Ohri and Faruqi reject the age structure hypothesis as a significant factor; they argue that patterns of discrimination occur whatever the level of qualifications; they suspend judgement on the hypothesis which links labour surplus with increased rates of discrimination; they argue that the regional and occupational factors contain elements which tend to counterbalance and are therefore not significant overall; and they call for more evidence on patterns of redundancy.

Their consideration of the evidence offers the conclusion that discrimination is a major factor in determining the patterns of employment and unemployment:

> regardless of whether one examines the situation of those blacks in employment, those skilled, unskilled or professional, those unemployed or indeed those on government-sponsored YTS, it must be concluded that blacks have been, and are, discriminated against at every level and in every sphere. (Ohri and Faruqi, 1988, p. 94)

Moreover, they assert in conclusion that 'racism and social discrimination accounts for most of the discrepancies in the employment statistics for black people'.

Controlled studies have been conducted at intervals that

involved the use of letters to employers which were identical with the exception of clues to ethnic identity. Smith (1977) describes the method as follows:

> Written or typed letters of application are sent for a sample of advertised jobs. Two applications are made for each job, one in the name of a white British applicant and the other in the name of an immigrant. Where both applicants are invited to an interview this is treated as a case of 'no discrimination' but where one applicant is invited to an interview and the other is not, this is treated as a case of discrimination. (Smith, 1977, p. 118)

Under these circumstances black minority applicants were discriminated against by about 30 per cent of employers. There was little difference between the levels of discrimination against different groups (West Indians 33 per cent, Indians 27 per cent and Pakistanis 30 per cent). There was clear evidence of differences between jobs in the levels of discrimination found, with the highest levels of discrimination occurring amongst higher status jobs. The applicants would have had no grounds for recognizing that discrimination had occurred on the basis of the letters they received.

The first waves of black migrants to Britain in the 1950s and 1960s suffered from processes of discrimination. Some found themselves working in jobs for which they were over-qualified, their formal qualifications sometimes, or often, not being recognized as equivalent to British qualifications, and those with skills which did not have formal accreditation were dissatisfied to discover that they could only obtain unskilled jobs (Patterson, 1965; Daniel, 1968; Humphry and John, 1971; Hiro, 1973; Lawrence, 1974). But what of Britain in the 1980s? Thirty years on, what is the significance of the processes of job recruitment and hiring and how do they impinge upon black people, upon the children and grand-children of the migrants of the 1950s and 1960s?

It is the practices and processes of recruitment, the criteria involved in the selection of new employees and in promotion, which are the key to the reproduction of inequalities in employment. These dimensions of work experience include the practical reasoning of those responsible for hiring new employees, and the routine procedures which are followed in selection.

In a study of managers in organizations, Jenkins (1986) documented the models held by recruiters of the workers which they preferred to employ (in other words, the criteria which they considered important in selection). He also examined the ways in which these matched their models of black and white workers and how this affected recruitment. Another feature of Jenkins's study was his analysis of the routines and practices which regulated the recruitment and promotion of workers. The economic context of the study, the recession of the early 1980s, was reflected in concern about its effects upon black workers. The project was conducted in the West Midlands and involved interviews with 172 managers (69 personnel specialists and 103 line managers) in the public sector, manufacturing and retailing. A detailed case study of one organization was also included in the research.

In considering selection criteria, Jenkins distinguished between *suitability* and *acceptability*. Whereas the suitability of employees was concerned with their skills and competence, their acceptability was related to a more general assessment of desirability, based upon personal judgements of social, cultural and other criteria. The interviews conducted by Jenkins made it clear that the concerns of managers with control of the workplace led to the development and interpretation of criteria for employment which were to the disadvantage of black workers. Jenkins concluded that 'Many criteria of acceptability are . . . profoundly ethnocentric.' Managers' judgements of the attributes of applicants' appearance, their social behaviour, style of speech and underlying attitudes, for example, revealed ethnocentric assumptions.

One of the features of judgement about potential employees which made the situation difficult to remedy was the informality of many criteria of acceptability. These criteria were often implicit, rather than explicit, and they were taken for granted rather than openly examined and analysed. The summary appeal by managers to their 'gut feeling' in the making of employment decisions epitomized the ethnocentric qualities of selection. Jenkins suggests that there are three major consequences of this state of affairs. First, the investigation of decisions and the reasoning behind them is made difficult. Second, the involvement of ethnocentrism and discrimination on racial grounds passes unchallenged into the process of selection of employees. Third, some of the criteria which are used to determine 'acceptibility' (such as English language competence, literacy, previous work experience) may be directly and indirectly discriminatory, and may thus 'tend to reproduce the collective disadvantage experienced by black workers' (p. 236).

These criteria of acceptability may also interact with ethnic stereotypes. Jenkins draws attention to two aspects of this: first, ethnic stereotypes may operate to stigmatize certain types of workers as less acceptable than others; and second, there may be some over-generalizations about black workers. An additional problem for black workers, or potential black workers, is that:

> given these managers' views on 'race relations' and the presence of black people in the United Kingdom . . . there is also the unfortunate likelihood that many of them will simply regard black people as an unacceptable presence, particularly in a time of high unemployment. Similar sentiments underlie the expression of the need to maintain 'a racial balance', or the frequently voiced opinion that 'nowadays it's the whites that are discriminated against'. (Jenkins, 1986, p. 236)

Jenkins sums up his discussion by noting that 'the situation can be encapsulated in two phrases: "the racism of acceptability" and "the acceptability of racism" ' (pp. 236–7). However, these processes, unexamined and uncritically applied, do not lead to auto-critique and reflexivity on the part of the managers, followed by self-correcting behaviour. Rather, they lead towards another case of 'blaming the victim':

> In each case the cause of the problem is popularly seen to be black workers themselves. On the one hand, they are seen to lack the personal attributes which might make them either more acceptable or acceptable outside their traditional labour-market ghettoes; on the other, the difficulties of the multi-ethnic situation are seen to be created not by racism, but by the 'unreasonable' demands and expectations of black workers. Either way, of course, it is black workers who lose ... (p. 237)

The organizational processes of recruitment tended to operate to the disadvantage of black workers. Jenkins draws attention to the informality of recruitment into employment and the corresponding absence of accountability. He also emphasizes the effects of 'internal search'. Since this method relies in particular upon word-of-mouth recruitment, thus giving priority to existing workers and their contacts, it minimizes the likelihood of some categories of potential employees hearing of the availability of work. Jenkins argues that 'in a number of respects, there seems little doubt that the widespread use of social networks in recruitment is a major factor in the production and reproduction of ethnic disadvantage in the labour market' (p. 238). A structural feature of the employment process mentioned by Jenkins is the 'organisational politics of recruitment', which does not allocate a major role to personnel work and which marginalizes equal opportunities procedures.

In conclusion, Jenkins suggests that:

> racism and discrimination remain virulent and black workers continue to suffer disadvantage as a consequence. Much of this discrimination is neither strikingly visible nor necessarily self-consciously prejudiced; some of it is not even deliberate. (p. 240)

Housing

The interaction of systems of discrimination and their accumulated effects over time can be seen through analysis of the changing situation of ethnic minorities in the housing market. Housing available to those migrating in the 1950s was commonly located in the inner areas of the large cities of Britain. These areas were in the process of being vacated by others seeking better accommodation in the suburbs or being rehoused through the expansion of council housing. Some areas had in the past been occupied by the middle classes and were at that time readily converted to multiple occupancy. Others were originally part of the nineteenth-century stock of housing which was built rapidly, and with minimal facilities, for working people. Whatever their origins and previous occupancy, these houses were commonly in the stages of decline but not entirely resistant to refurbishment by their new occupants.

The occupation of accommodation by the new migrants in the 1950s and 1960s was shaped by processes of discrimination, and there were a number of reports in different areas of Britain of landlords operating a 'colour bar' (Luthera, 1988). Controlled studies of discrimination in housing were conducted in the 1960s and the 1970s (Smith, 1977). The method was summarized by Smith as follows:

> The tests were carried out by actors working in pairs, and for each test one of the pair was white while the other was Indian, Pakistani, West Indian or Greek ... The bulk of the house-purchase tests involved personal visits to estate agents, but a few were telephone inquiries about houses which had been advertised. In the case of rented accommodation, the tester replied by telephone to advertisements in the newspapers. (Smith, 1977, p. 285)

The level of discrimination revealed in these tests was high (Table 3.2), but the Race Relations Act 1968 may have had an impact since there was a notable decrease in discrimination in the 1973 study compared with that conducted in 1967.

Two related processes are revealed by the distinction in

Table 3.2 between 'different treatment' and 'inferior treatment'. The investigators concluded that in the house purchase tests, Asian and West Indian people were offered houses which were inferior in 12 per cent of the cases, and houses which were different but not clearly inferior in 17 per cent of the cases.

Table 3.2 *Level of discrimination in 1967 and 1973 for house purchase and rented accommodation*

Type of housing	Discrimination against West Indian tester in 1967 (%)	Discrimination against West Indian and Asian testers in 1973 (%)
Rented accommodation (telephone)	62	27
Rented accommodation (personal)	75	NA
House purchase (personal)	64	17 (different treatment) 12 (inferior treatment)

Discrimination in housing and in the allocation of mortgages was one of a number of factors (such as low wages and unemployment) which set the pattern of housing for ethnic minorities through the 1970s and 1980s. Moreover, the actions of 'gatekeepers' with responsibility for the allocation of housing were significant not only in the private sector. As housing conditions changed and 'slum clearance' progressed through the 1970s and 1980s local authority housing policies became an element in the pattern of housing for ethnic minorities.

A number of cases of discrimination in the housing policies of local authorities were investigated by the Commission for Racial Equality in the 1980s. Discrimination in housing was found in Tower Hamlets Borough Council and Liverpool City Council in 1988 (CRE, 1990). Such discrimination by local authorities has affected the quality of local authority housing available to ethnic minorities. The effects of discrimination and the practices involved are indicated by the Commission for Racial Equality's findings against the London Borough of Tower Hamlets following its investigations in 1988. One of the areas of concern for the Commission was the allocation of families to particular housing estates when they were rehoused. However, three of the findings were concerned with homelessness, which included reference to the way an emergency housing case was treated, the Council's policy on separated families, and the length of stay in bed and breakfast accommodation. The Commission notes:

> Homelessness is a growing problem in the UK, and in London it has reached levels that should be unacceptable in any civilised society. The wretched conditions and the constant insecurity of the homeless have been well publicised. What is less well known is that ethnic minorities are represented amongst the homeless at disproportionately high levels and have suffered racial discrimination as well as all the other problems associated with homelessness. (CRE, 1989a, p. 42)

Racial attacks

The incidence of racial attacks and racial harassment has been increasingly recognized as a serious problem as surveys from the Home Office and other official agencies have accumulated to reinforce the reports from ethnic minority communities. The targets for racial incidents are commonly Asian and Afro-Caribbean people, who are 50 times and 36 times respectively

95

more likely than white people to be the victims of racial attacks. Other ethnic minority communities including Chinese, Jewish, and Vietnamese also suffer from harassment.

The official figures now cover some of the major multi-ethnic areas of the country. Data from the Metropolitan Police record 2,179 racial incidents in 1987 (compared with 1,733 in 1986), with particularly intensive problems in the London boroughs of Tower Hamlets and Newham. In the West Midlands, 754 racial incidents were reported to the police in 1987. In the same year there were reports of 217 racial incidents in Strathclyde. These statistics include assaults, abuse or threatening behaviour, criminal damage, and fire-raising (Home Office, 1989).

The official figures underestimate the frequency of racial incidents. Independent surveys have reported substantially greater numbers of racial incidents than those recorded in official statistics. A survey conducted in Leeds estimated a level of racial harassment of about ten times that predicted from Home Office data; a survey in Glasgow found that more than half of the Asian sample had suffered from damage to their property and four-fifths had experienced racial abuse; a survey in the London Borough of Newham reported that one in four ethnic minority people living in the borough had experienced racial harassment within the previous year.

Surveys of racial harassment and racial incidents are from urban areas. Rural areas, including those with very few, or even no, minority ethnic families are also the location of racial incidents. The prevalence of racist graffiti in even the remotest parts of Britain is an indicator of the kinds of response given to black people when they visit such areas.

The effects of frequent, low-level racial harassment are persistent and serious. As a Home Office report notes:

There may ... be a tendency to view some minor incidents as unpleasant but essentially trivial anti-social behaviour that does not warrant any special attention. We should make it clear from the outset that we do not share this view. Racially motivated murder is – fortunately – an extremely rare occurrence; but in some areas of the country many people of minority ethnic origin will have some experience of the less serious types of racial incidents: jostling in the street, racial abuse by children and teenagers, insulting behaviour by neighbours, the dumping of rubbish or the daubing of racist graffiti on their property, for example. It is important to recognise that, when repeated over time, apparently trivial incidents of this kind create an insidious atmosphere of racial harassment and intimidation ... We are in no doubt that these apparently 'trivial' racial incidents are seriously damaging the quality of life for members of the minority communities. (Home Office, 1989, para. 11)

This review of four major aspects of British life which have effects upon the qualities of experience of ethnic minorities (immigration, employment, housing, and safety on the streets) indicates that, on the basis of official data and controlled investigations, racial discrimination is significant. Moreover, it is clear that there are progressive, or accumulating, effects of discrimination which may have direct and indirect consequences for education. Discrimination in the field of employment affects income, which in turn affects the quality of housing available. The location of housing may influence access to social networks which in turn may have consequences for employment. The location of housing is a factor in providing access to schools, and schools vary considerably in their available resources and material condition. The resources available to a family through income and housing are significant dimensions of the quality of educational experience.

There are implications here (made clear as much by the analysis of the processes involved as by their outcomes) for teachers individually and collectively. For example, the summary above points to some of the particular problems of pastoral care for ethnic minority pupils (which may include problems arising from the separation of families through the immigration laws). There is a need to exercise care with the criteria which are formally and informally employed in the academic assessment of pupils. Criteria considered in more general social and personal evaluations of pupils required in references and reports may also need careful consideration. The issues of discipline and bullying, especially with reference to the racial dimension, should not be neglected. When attention is given to the social dynamics and ethos of the school, and the destinations of school-leavers, the value of education about race and discrimination for all pupils becomes apparent.

These dimensions of education can be clarified by consideration of evidence about pupils and teachers with reference to the perceptions and awareness of ethnic issues, and their effects upon interaction in schools.

Schools and racism

Pupils

Studies of the development of ethnic awareness and ethnic identity amongst children reveal the emergence of ethnic awareness and the expression of negative reactions to some ethnic minority groups at between 3 and 5 years of age (Davey, 1983; Milner, 1983; Aboud, 1988). Where such studies have involved comparison of white children with ethnic minorities there have been clear differences between the groups, with white children demonstrating higher degrees of ethnic intolerance than ethnic minority children. Thus by the time children begin nursery school or enter primary school, they possess emergent values which can take on a progressively sharper and more negative form, or which can be modified through their educational experiences.

In a survey by the Commission for Racial Equality, a number of instances of racial harassment amongst primary school pupils were reported. These included the case of a 7-year-old girl who suffered from persistent name-calling by a white child of the same age, and who was beaten up by that girl's older sister. In a similar case the mother of a 9-year-old

Asian girl who had been the victim of regular racial abuse and bullying was attacked by the parents of the child responsible for the bullying (CRE, 1988).

Visits to primary schools in predominantly white areas by HM Inspectors have led to comments about the insularity of some staff and reports of expressions of hostility towards black people by some primary school pupils. Discussions with pupils during visits to secondary schools in predominantly white areas revealed low levels of understanding of the situation of ethnic minorities, together with a considerable degree of antagonism from some pupils (Swann Report, Chapter 5, Annex C).

The development of hostile attitudes towards members of ethnic minority groups may thus occur in areas which are predominantly white. It does not depend upon immediate contact and there are clear differences between groups in the degrees of antagonism towards others. Such perspectives, and the corresponding misunderstandings, could be left to be reproduced through peer group influence and on into the next generation. On the other hand, schools could develop rules and codes of conduct for their pupils and an appropriate curriculum which could more appropriately educate their pupils for life in a multicultural society.

Teachers

The existence of stereotypical responses to ethnic minority pupils by teachers has been a contentious issue. The construction of stereotypes, such as that of the submissive Asian girl, the striving and over-ambitious Asian boy, or the boisterous West Indian child whose energies and dedication can be channelled into sport but not into academic subjects, appears to be a flexible process. Some notions of what is typical for particular groups have changed through the decades, but whatever the stereotype, it does reveal assumptions about the relative perceptions of particular groups. The extent to which teachers hold differential expectations of particular types of pupil and the effects of these expectations are of considerable relevance for schools. They may have consequences for pupils' attainment both directly and indirectly. For example, they may work directly through the qualities of interaction in the class-room, affecting the kind of educational experience of pupils. They may work with equal effect as a result of decisions about banding and streaming. They may have an indirect impact through the teachers' interactions with parents in the normal course of parent evenings and home–school links.

In a study of inner-city schools, Tizard *et al.* (1988) found that fewer black than white parents were given information about their children's educational performance. Answers given by teachers to the question 'What has been your experience of West Indian parents?' revealed that a number of teachers had stereotypes of these parents, with only 13 per cent refraining from offering generalizations. Seventy per cent offered negative evaluations, asserting, for example, that West Indian parents were too concerned about their children's education, expected too high a standard of achievement, and were too authoritarian at home. However, about one-third of the teachers gave positive evaluations of West Indian parents, some of these similar to the characteristics evaluated as negative by others, such as 'keen on education'.

The issues of the effects of teacher expectations upon pupils was raised in the 1960s through a series of projects and, in particular, as a result of research conducted by Rosenthal and Jacobson (1968). Rosenthal and Jacobson's study was based upon children in an elementary school in a working-class neighbourhood. Teachers were encouraged to believe that certain pupils were expected to show marked gains in achievement in the forthcoming school year. Rosenthal and Jacobson argued that these pupils made considerable gains on a number of educational measures during the year, gains which were not matched by those pupils who had not been identified as likely to do well. A further finding from the study was that teacher perceptions of the pupils who were expected to do well were more socially positive than those of their counterparts who were not expected to do well. However, if children did well who were not expected to do well, there were negative consequences: their teachers perceived them socially in negative terms. Close analysis of Rosenthal and Jacobson's data revealed that this effect was largely a result of responses to children in lower streams.

The design of Rosenthal and Jacobson's study is in an experimental tradition which sets up a stimulus ('teacher expectations') and measures a response ('pupil performance'): thus it sheds little light on the process of teaching or the qualities of teacher behaviour in the classroom. Furthermore, the results of Rosenthal and Jacobson's study have been subject to considerable criticism, with alternative interpretations of the data and spirited defences by the authors (for example, Grieger, 1971; Rosenthal, 1972). Nevertheless there has been an accumulation of evidence from related studies, with different designs and samples (Rosenthal and Rosnow, 1969), which supports the general idea of the impact of teacher expectations upon pupil performance. These have included investigations which clarified how teacher expectancy effects operate. In one study, in which teachers were observed, there were overt and dramatic differences in the teaching styles adopted for pupils expected to do well in comparison with the remainder (Rosenthal, 1969). In another study the grounds for teacher expectations were investigated, together with how teachers organized their classrooms and responded to pupils (Rist, 1970, cited by Bryman, 1988). Thus there are good grounds for considering that teacher expectations may have some impact upon the educational performance of their pupils.

A more recent study by Green (1985) brought together themes of teacher attitudes, teaching styles, and their impacts upon pupils. Green's research was based upon 70 teachers and their 1,814 pupils in three middle schools and three junior schools. The teachers were all white British nationals and the pupils mixed groups, with about one-half of European origin, about one-quarter of Asian background, and about one-quarter of Afro-Caribbean background. There were marginally more boys in the sample (52 per cent) than girls (48 per cent). The central questions to Green's research were:

(i) Are teachers' gender, ethnocentrism and types of attitudes towards education associated with the use they make of different modes of teaching?

and

(ii) Is that teaching correlated with the child's level of self-concept?

The data collected by Green to evaluate these issues included questionnaires, interviews, and evidence from close observation of what happened in the classrooms.

There were marked differences between the qualities of the educational experience received by pupils of different ethnic background in some teachers' classrooms. For example, pupils of Afro-Caribbean background in the classrooms of highly intolerant teachers were likely to gain less praise, less attention to their ideas, less direct teaching, and less time to initiate contribution to class discussions than their white counterparts. However, pupils of Afro-Caribbean origin were likely to be more subject to direction and control than white pupils in the classrooms of ethnocentric teachers. With such evidence, one of Green's conclusions is:

Boys and girls of different ethnic origins taught in the same multi-ethnic classroom by the same teacher are likely to receive widely different educational experiences, some elements of which may be differentially related to the teacher's gender, the types of education, and when present, extreme levels of ethnocentrism. (Green, 1985, p. 53)

The impact of teachers and teaching styles upon pupils' self-concepts was also analysed. Green argued that teachers' attitudes affected the educational environment through their teaching styles, and that this had a differential effect upon the self-concepts of pupils:

. . . within those classes taught by highly intolerant teachers, boys of European origin recorded a level of self-concept which is very significantly higher than those of boys and girls of Asian and of West Indian origins but which is not significantly different from that of girls of European origin. Within those classes taught by highly tolerant teachers there are no statistically significant differences in self-concept levels. (Green, 1985, p. 50)

Procedures and practices

Decisions by teachers about the rules and procedures of their schools, including such routines as recording the names of pupils, regulations about school uniforms, and customs on the provision of school meals, may have differential impacts upon pupils in a multi-ethnic context. The influence of differential expectations, and of general notions of acceptability and suitability (which may parallel the decisions of personnel officers discussed above), may become amplified through decisions about banding and streaming. Allocations to bands, streams and work-groups can be the means by which patterns of differential treatment of pupils are not only reinforced but may have a long-term impact. These are critical aspects of the structures of schools, which determine examination entry and examination performance. They also regulate to some extent the patterns of interaction between different groups of pupils and may contribute to the determination of important features of the social life and ethos of the school.

A study by Eggleston (1986) charts the entry to two secondary schools of pupils of different ethnic minority background, with broadly similar educational profiles, and their subsequent segregation through allocation to different streams. Some of the decisions about streaming were clearly not made on the basis of internal examination performance alone; other forms of judgement were taken as the overriding criteria in some cases, and the pattern which emerged was of ethnic minority pupils being allocated to lower streams than white pupils. Research by Tomlinson and Smith (1989) into 18 multi-ethnic schools suggests that white children have a greater probability of gaining access to high-level courses than black children. In an earlier paper based upon the study Tomlinson reported that:

> [the] evidence . . . suggests that option choice procedures, as they have developed in comprehensive schools over the past twenty-five years, can have the effect of disadvantaging groups who are racially or ethnically different, although membership of such groups and any educational disadvantages, obviously overlaps with class and gender groupings and disadvantages. (Tomlinson, 1987, p. 94)

The effects upon the informal social groupings of pupils as a result of differential treatment of the white and black pupils in banding and streaming can be significant. Friendship patterns, mutual understanding, sharing of leisure facilities within and outside the school, and collaborative or competitive networks can be shaped by the structures imposed through the school day. An American study of school organization in a multi-ethnic context makes this particularly clear. Hallinan and Williams (1989) conclude:

> . . . School organizational characteristics can . . . affect inter-racial friendship formation. The distribution of students across organizational units can effectively integrate a school population by ensuring a reasonable mix of black and white students within instructional groups. When this occurs, inter-racial interactions take place by chance as well as by choice. Students have the opportunity to get to know cross-race peers better, to observe existing similarities, and to develop new similarities that may transcend the racial barrier to positive effect.
>
> On the other hand, the assignment of students to tracks can effectively resegregate a desegregated school. (Hallinan and Williams, p. 77)

The research summarized above, on the development of pupils' ethnic identity, their understanding of ethnic differences, together with the analysis of the effects of teachers' perceptions of pupils and their classroom interaction and the effects of school routines, procedures and structures such as banding and streaming, points towards the need for systematic responses by schools to the presence of racism and discrimination. The rationale for a 'whole-school' response rather than a supplementary or crisis-management approach should be clear. The next section explores two aspects of responses to the issue: teaching about race and race relations and dealing with racial incidents and harassment.

Teaching about race and race relations

There are sets of beliefs which have a core assumption about treating people as equals. Some are based upon the conviction that all people are equal in the eyes of God. Others, while not derived from faith in a supreme being, are linked with a complex set of ideas about people and equality which tends to stress mutual respect, democratic participation in society, the meeting of basic needs and a sense of community (Baker, 1987). When set against these belief systems, differential responses to people based upon certain arbitrarily selected, physical characteristics appear (amongst other things) to be decidedly odd. However, it is not oddity, nor the corresponding incompetence in social and educational affairs, which is at the core of the educational challenge to racism: it is injustice.

As a challenge to injustice, an educational perspective which challenges racism inevitably intersects with other themes such as religious discrimination or inequalities resulting from gender or social class differences. These are, by now, traditional concerns in British education, as Troyna and Williams contend (1986, p. 91). Thus the grounding for teaching about race and race relations is broadly based upon religious, social, and ethical judgements. Halstead (1988) argues that there are five indispensable components of 'teaching children about racial justice'. These are:

1. moral training;
2. the transmission of knowledge, understanding and attitudes;
3. the development of moral commitment;
4. the development of critical awareness;

105

5. the development of political understanding. (Halstead, 1988, p. 164)

When located in this traditional context, representation of the purpose and themes of teaching about race and race relations may seem unproblematic. However, the issue is also controversial; there is more than a trace of volatility in the substance and a threat of instability in the context of teaching, given the evidence about children's and young people's attitudes. Moreover, the combination of the need to enhance understanding of complex social processes together with the development of moral evaluations offers a formidable challenge. The content, the form, the pedagogy, the materials, and the assessment of such teaching pose a range of problems.

Studies of the development of ethnic identity amongst young children have led to recommendations about what could be taught to young children to reduce the development of prejudice. Aboud (1988) offers an approach for 4- to 7-year-olds based upon two assumptions. These are as follows:

1. Prejudice is based on a polarized and simple dichotomy of positive versus negative emotions. A greater differentiation among emotions reduces prejudice.
2. Prejudice is based on an egocentric judgement that only one way of experiencing the world is the correct way. Learning the many ways of being right reduces prejudice. (Aboud, 1988, p. 132)

Aboud also reports studies which have led to prejudice reduction amongst older children. These employed a range of activities designed to facilitate judgements by children on internal attributes rather than external attributes, drawing attention to between-group similarities and within-group differences, and fostering acceptance of views which are different from their own.

These examples rest upon a North American tradition which focuses upon the individual and her or his perceptions. The discussion of racism above leads to consideration of something more than attitudes, prejudice and stereotypes. It involves understanding social patterns and routines which lead to discrimination, together with recognition of the interaction of such structures and practices and the formation of personal understanding. If this more complex understanding of the issues is coupled with the recognition that the education of children in secondary school is the preparatory stage before entry into a wider participation in life, the task of educating young people about race and race relations seems daunting.

An example of a course specifically designed as a unit for teaching about race and community relations is that devised at Shipley College. Integral features of the Shipley approach are that it was student-centred and participative, and that it involved attempts to get students to explore the links between their experiences and the wider economic and political context. The course was a 26-hour programme, with a main purpose of 'attempting to explore the link between the specific experiences of individuals and the economic and political context in which they occur' (Robson, 1987, pp. 48–9). As part of a communications skills programme, the course was intended to enable 'young people to develop the attitudes, knowledge and communication skills to start to unlearn their personal racism and to begin to undo institutional racism' (Robson, 1987, p. 49). The approach of the course was not intended to be divisive or to trigger guilt reactions but to create 'a climate of mutual support and critical thought in the classroom' (p. 49). This approach clearly emphasizes the process of learning while operating within a flexible framework. Robson stresses:

'the development of an anti-racist curriculum as a *process* involving students in developing the skills of enquiry and critical thought, rather than ... the imposition of a finished product devised by teachers. (pp. 49–50)

The approach can be clarified by reference to what Robson identifies as dilemmas in anti-racist education. These are represented as:

1. the cognitive vs. the affective approach (emotions vs. under-standing and analysis);
2. emphasis upon racism or the combination of racism with other issues such as race, sex, and class;
3. the interpersonal vs. the institutional and structural level of analysis ('solidarity or sympathy').

This set of alternatives in effect maps out the range of the course, which included evidence about racism and discussion of attitudes, interpersonal relations and action, the latter including what happens in institutional contexts (Figure 2). The emphasis upon solidarity demonstrates the way in which this approach considers that the relationship between groups (within the classroom and outside) is important – not toler-ance, pity or sympathy, but solidarity and support.

The course does not employ a social-psychological model of racism which leads to an emphasis upon white guilt or potentially divisive course outcomes. The criticisms of 'Race Awareness Training' (Gurnah, 1984; Sivanandan, 1985), which concentrate upon 'psychological' approaches, their arou-sal of guilt, and their abstraction from structural analysis, do not apply to the content of the Shipley course, nor to the teaching process adopted. The active, co-operative approach at Shipley rests upon a more positive model of the learner than that implied by Gurnah and Sivanandan. The course also contrasts with approaches to preparation for life which stress individual enterprise in the market-place, while maintaining a silence about the political world and the possibilities of collec-tive action or social inventiveness.

Responding to racial incidents

The analysis above of the ways in which discrimination may occur has drawn attention to the effects of practices and procedures. In earlier chapters there have been passing refer-ences to issues such as the ethos of the school, discipline, rules and routines. Whereas the curriculum is undoubtedly

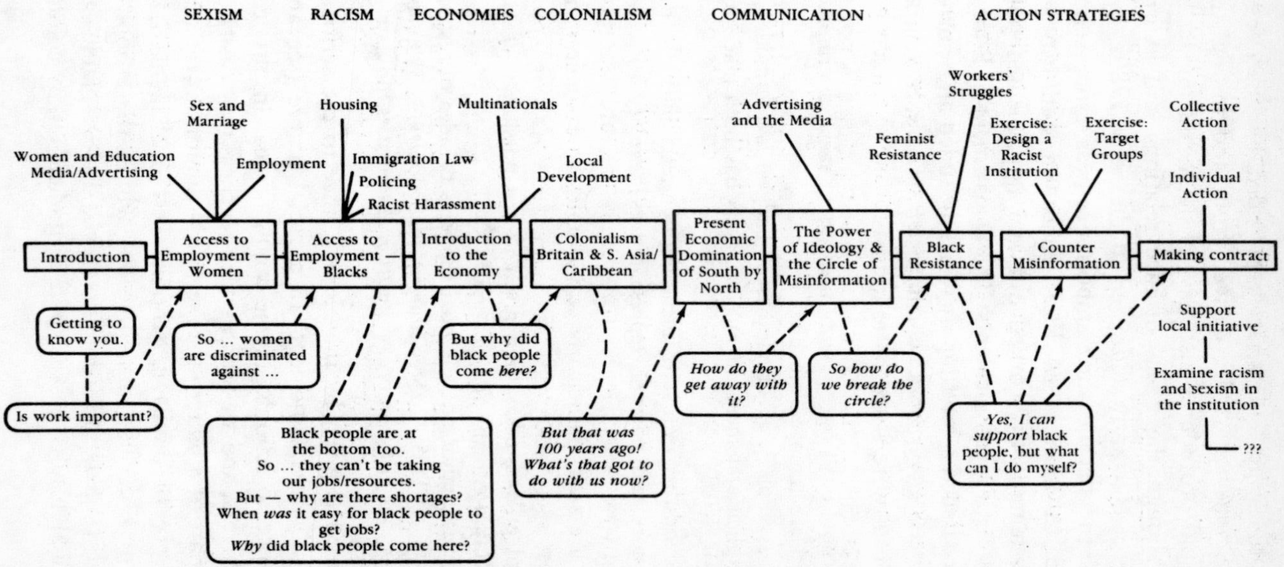

Figure 2 Course outline for teaching race.

SEXISM RACISM ECONOMIES COLONIALISM COMMUNICATION ACTION STRATEGIES

Women and Education
Media/Advertising

Sex and Marriage
Employment

Housing
Immigration Law
Policing
Racist Harassment

Multinationals
Local Development

Advertising and the Media

Feminist Resistance
Workers' Struggles

Exercise: Design a Racist Institution
Exercise: Target Groups

Collective Action
Individual Action

Introduction

Access to Employment Women

Access to Employment Blacks

Introduction to the Economy

Colonialism Britain & S. Asia/Caribbean

Present Economic Domination of South by North

The Power of Ideology & the Circle of Misinformation

Black Resistance

Counter Misinformation

Making contract

Support local initiative
Examine racism and sexism in the institution

???

Getting to know you.

Is work important?

So ... women are discriminated against ...

Black people are at the bottom too.
So ... they can't be taking our jobs/resources.
But — why are there shortages?
When was it easy for black people to get jobs?
Why did black people come here?

But why did black people come here?

But that was 100 years ago! What's that got to do with us now?

How do they get away with it?

How do we break the circle?

So how do we break the circle?

Yes, I can support black people, but what can I do myself?

Source: Robson (1987)

an influential aspect of what is provided by a school, the communications which are derived from and through rules, practices and procedures also have a significant impact upon pupils. Although the issues of race relations and racism in school were reluctantly addressed in the early 1980s, by the middle of the decade their importance was more seriously considered. A number of local education authorities and schools systematically worked out and implemented policies for dealing with racial incidents. The Department of Education and Science issued a brief report which included an itemization of 'aspects of any school which foster good race relations'. These aspects were listed as follows:

a. the school deals openly with incidents of racial discrimination;
b. graffiti are removed quickly;
c. racist symbols (e.g., on clothes or badges) are forbidden;
d. an explicit statement on race relations has been made by the school;
e. discussions between staff (including non-teaching staff), pupils, governors and parents' representatives have led to a 'whole school view';
f. there are staff, particularly senior staff, from ethnic minority groups;
g. careful attention has been given to the possibility of bias in curriculum content and materials;
h. the general ethos of the school supports the idea of respect for all pupils. (DES, *Race Relations in Schools: A Summary of Discussions in Five Local Education Authorities*, no date, p. 7)

The emphasis given by the Home Office to the seriousness of apparently trivial incidents of a racial nature (see above) has relevance to schools. Name-calling, casual insults, covert physical threats, and sly kicks, which teachers may easily overlook, are part of a pattern that seriously diminishes the quality of experience of pupils in schools. Left unchallenged, such incidents may develop into divisions within the school, and subsequent tragedy (Macdonald *et al.*, 1989). Name-calling and personal insults based upon a student's skin colour or culture are not only an attack on an individual in isolation, but also on that person's family and community. The context which gives such actions meaning includes a known situation of racial harassment, attacks on the street, and discrimination in the wider social world. Recognition of this led to the increasing acceptance of the need to be aware of, record, monitor, and deal with racial incidents and harassment in schools as the 1980s progressed.

A check on terminology and language

The outline of the concepts and processes of racism and racialization in the introductory section of this chapter, and the examples which followed, reveal the multi-dimensional and fluid nature of the issues. The passing references to volatility and guilt in the discussion of teaching about race are hints that the unintended consequences of raising the issues at all may be displays of hostility, defensiveness, evasion and conflict within the groups being taught. In earlier chapters, attempts have been made to reveal the nature of evidence, together with conclusions about the presence of racism or the effects of other factors which disadvantage people. Earlier chapters too have tried to reveal the differences between the discourse of competing approaches to education for a multicultural society. These differing strands of earlier arguments can be brought together with questions about how the concept of racism is appropriately used. There are two issues in this instance: first, are there other processes which should be part of the discussion? (please note the questioning of a single-factor argument); and second, what are the educational and policy consequences of the use of language which stresses racism rather than that which avoids use of the term?

The question about the inter-relationship of different processes can be expanded by a comment of Banton about the sociology of racial relations:

> It is possible to discuss the sociology of racial relations without using the word 'racism'. Other words, like racial discrimination, prejudice, incitement, doctrine, ethnocentrism, and so on, are sufficient for almost any purpose. (Banton, 1988, p. 28)

Careful analysis of the processes of, say, economic change and restructuring, and discrimination which incorporates aspects of gender and social class, reveals the place of 'racism' within a network of forces rather than in isolation.

This does not necessarily diminish the significance of racism, especially when historical factors are taken into account. Just as the layouts of city streets today may reveal medieval field patterns, so the patterns of social hierarchy within societies may reveal earlier structures of domination. This is particularly the case in those societies which suffered the early impacts of colonialism, where most of the indigenous people were wiped out and the African slave trade was used for substitute labour (Latin American and Caribbean societies). Britain's social structures were not separate from these global processes, but the need to identify carefully the nature of the circumstances, and the history of divisions and conflicts within society, prompts circumspection in the use of the summary term 'racism'.

Caution in the use of the term may also arise through pragmatism. The consideration of discrimination generally, the introduction of discussion of stereotypes indirectly (e.g., with reference to those with disabilities), comparative analysis of inequalities (e.g., gender divisions), and historical discussion of religious conflict (e.g., in Northern Ireland) may lead to a greater understanding of issues of racial discrimination and conflict than an approach based entirely upon direct confrontations. There is also an irony in education about race in that, since guilt figures prominently in some people's socialization, so much so that some appear to be seeking the experience of guilt, the educator may be leading the student away from guilt rather than towards it. The issue of personal responsibility, the tactics of avoidance and evasion which may arise, and the necessity to be sensitive to the visibility of minorities (and other pressures upon them) demonstrate the advantages of an educational discourse on these issues which is low-key and facilitative rather than confrontational and paralysing.

Conclusions

The main strand of the argument in this chapter has been that the issue of racism in British society warrants serious attention. The evidence on the limited but major aspects of citizenship considered above demonstrates the presence and continuing impact of racism upon people's lives. Some of the ways in which central government (e.g., through the Home Office's concern with racial attacks, and the Department of Education and Science's attention to racial harassment in schools) began to address the issue in the 1980s and regarded the matter as increasingly serious have been demonstrated. Ways in which the issues can be tackled in schools include classroom styles, banding and streaming, and school rules and procedures. There are also issues for the curriculum, through cross-curricular themes and teaching about race and race relations.

The controversial nature of these issues and the challenges which they bring to existing practice in education have led to episodes of conflict. Four of these episodes are considered in Chapter 4.

4 Case studies in controversy

Introduction

There have been intermittent incidents and episodes within schools or communities, and between different tiers of government which have revealed the complexity of issues and intensity of conflict following the introduction of changes to achieve education for cultural diversity. The purpose of this chapter is to review some of the most critical of these incidents. Each has unique features and each concerns different levels of conflict, so there can be no attempt to offer a general prescription or lesson-guide following their analysis. Nevertheless, consideration of the issues, the processes of debate and their resolution may lead us towards some points of reference for the future development and implementation of education. They may also serve as markers which reveal the direction and extent of educational progress.

Four major episodes of conflict are considered in approximate chronological order. The first involved a headteacher, his local authority, parents and the community. The second is an account of a struggle by a group of parents to prevent their children from attending a school which had a significant number of black British pupils. The third describes the responses of central government to the attempts by a local authority to introduce a systematic policy for the implementation of racial equality in education. The fourth concerns the tragic circumstances of an Asian pupil killed on school premises, and the subsequent review and reporting of the context of the situation.

114

The development of each of these episodes was such that they had ramifications for more than those directly involved. The consequences were felt in other communities, schools and local authorities; indeed, these events can be said to have had something in common, in that they each achieved national significance. Another shared feature was that they became the subject of intense reporting through the media. The representation of these episodes in newspapers and on television and radio became part of the situation, to be dealt with by those involved. More significantly, in some cases the discrepancies between certain press reports and the events, the policies, or the recommendations following investigation were considerable. The final section of this chapter considers the media representation of the episodes.

The local authority, the headteacher, parents and the community – the Honeyford affair

Bradford Local Education Authority had a reputation for progressive educational adaptation to its ethnic minority pupils in the 1960s and 1970s, and responded to the presence of migrants in the post-war period with a series of initiatives, most notably through the provision of language centres. In the 1960s the local authority began a policy of transporting ethnic minority pupils in the inner-city areas to suburban schools (bussing) to ensure their dispersal. The criterion employed as an 'acceptable' percentage of ethnic minority pupils altered as the population changed but eventually, following considerable debate and recognition of its discriminatory nature, the policy was abandoned at the end of the 1970s. The 1960s and the 1970s were also a period of increasing participation of the ethnic minority communities in the life of the city, economically, socially and politically. Some were elected as councillors in local elections, and there was an increase in group activity through the formation of new associations and committees (Halstead, 1988).

115

In the early 1980s there was a move in the local authority's approach to ethnic and community relations towards the implementation of a systematic scheme to promote equality of opportunity and to eliminate racial discrimination. The emerging policy included employment, ethnic monitoring, consultation with the minority ethnic communities and the introduction of racism awareness training. The authority's policy statement (approved in late 1981) asserted that:

> Bradford has both a multiracial and multicultural population and ... all sections of the community have an equal right to the maintenance of their distinctive identities and loyalties of culture, language, religion and custom.

In late 1982 the local authority distributed a memorandum entitled *Education for a Multicultural Society: Provision for Pupils of Ethnic Minority Communities*. The document's major concern was with the procedures and routines of schools and their effects on ethnic minority pupils. The general framework of the educational policy, of which this was a part, was provided in a statement from the Directorate of Educational Services. There were four general aims of education in Bradford:

1. To seek ways of preparing all children and young people for life in a multicultural society.
2. To counter racism and racist attitudes, and the inequalities and discrimination which result from them.
3. To build on and develop the strengths of cultural and linguistic diversity.
4. To respond sensitively to the special needs of minority groups.

The memorandum on provision for pupils of ethnic minority communities provided guidelines which were based upon the requirements of the Education Acts, while at the same time recognizing the experiences of ethnic minority pupils and the range of approaches which had been developed in schools. The issues covered included school and community, parental rights (with reference to information to parents, assemblies and religious education), and culture (including school uniform, jewellery, physical education, school meals and the recording of names). The guidance on school uniform permitted traditional dress ('In cases where pupils wish to wear traditional dress, parents should be asked to provide this dress in the school colours.'). The guidance on jewellery noted, 'The Sikh kara (steel bracelet worn on the right wrist) and the Muslim tawiz (a string with a small bag or box attached worn around the arm, neck or abdomen) are not jewellery and children must be allowed to wear them if their parents wish them to do so.' The document's major concern was with the procedures and routines of schools, with the intention of ensuring that they did not discriminate against ethnic minority pupils.

Also in 1982, Bradford Local Education Authority established a working party which included wide representation from the churches and religious groups in the city (including a range of Christian denominations) to design an agreed religious education syllabus. The recommendations of the group were published as an Agreed Syllabus for Religious Education in 1983. The introduction, consistent with the general aims of education quoted above, stated:

> ... the Authority feels that Bradford, rich in a diversity of faiths and cultures, needs to assert that the major religions, Hinduism, Islam, Judaism, Sikhism as well as Christianity, have an equal right to the maintenance of their distinctive identities and loyalties of culture, language, religion and custom; furthermore their rich diversity should be seen as contributing to the life of the whole community. (Bradford MDC, 1983, p. 1)

The syllabus which followed included coverage of the five major faiths referred to in the introduction.

Later in 1983, a memorandum concerned with racist behaviour in schools was sent to headteachers. This memorandum covered the identification of racist behaviour and procedures for the recording of racist incidents. Schools were required to develop policies on dealing with such incidents,

117

record them, and to report them to the local authority. Some headteachers resisted implementation of the memorandum, and the local branch of the Association of Headteachers formally voted against its implementation (Halstead, 1988).

One Bradford headteacher (Ray Honeyford) was prompted by some of these local (and national) developments to write letters and articles questioning and challenging the educational policies which were beginning to be implemented. Honeyford's articles appeared in a number of publications in the next few years, including *The Times Educational Supplement*, *Salisbury Review*, *The Spectator*, and *The Head Teachers' Review*. Some were subsequently republished in other sources as reaction to them grew.

Honeyford's articles included criticism of Bradford's policies, opposition to multicultural and anti-racist education, and remarks about Britain's ethnic minority communities. The main features of his argument about educational provision were that immigrants have a responsibility to adapt to the country to which they move, that the school does not have any responsibility for cultural maintenance (which should be the responsibility of the family), and that ethnic minority pupils should be taught British culture (not about the countries of their parents or other forebears). He argued that a critical approach to British history should not be adopted. His view on educational underachievement was that it was primarily caused by parents, and that the lack of encouragement by West Indian parents was particularly notable.

Honeyford's two articles in *The Times Educational Supplement* in 1982 drew considerable critical reaction in the correspondence columns. Locally, they led to an interview with the Director of Education and the Chairman of Bradford's Educational Services Committee, and an exchange of letters with Bradford's educational directorate. They also engaged the concern of Bradford's Council for Mosques. However, an article published in the *Salisbury Review* in early 1984 resulted in a stronger degree of intervention by the local authority, and the mobilization of a parents' group at Honeyford's school. These were the early moves in a chain of reactions and counter-reactions which led to his suspension, reinstatement, and then early retirement at the end of 1985 (Halstead, 1988).

The action by parents began with a meeting and calls for Honeyford's dismissal. Later stages of the action included marches, demonstrations and boycotts of the school in late 1985 which effectively reduced those pupils attending to as few as one-fifth, and not more than one-half, of those on the roll (Halstead, 1988). The ensuing conflict embroiled trades union branches, organizations in the minority ethnic communities, and political groups on the far right. Reporting of the events spread on a national and international scale.

The language employed by Honeyford and the rhetorical devices of his articles were neither low-key nor analytical. He conveyed his condemnations of some of those with whom he disagreed, and questioned their integrity polemically, by means of negative metaphors. For example, he referred to 'a group of people who have been called the "multi-ethnic brigade"' and continued, 'They claim to be concerned for the welfare of ethnic minorities but ...' (Honeyford, 1983). In the same article he referred to 'the fanatical determination of multi-ethnic "experts"' (with reference to guidelines for the evaluation of books) and to 'teachers building a career by jumping on the latest educational bandwagon'.

His comments about ethnic minorities as communities and individuals shared similar characteristics. For example, in one article he referred to 'a half-educated and volatile Sikh', to '(t)he hysterical political temperament of the Indian sub-continent', and asserted that 'The roots of black educational failure are, in reality, located in West Indian family structure and values ...' (Honeyford, 1984, p. 31).

Halstead argues that Honeyford's articles caused a breach with the local education authority in four ways. First, they were critical of most of the local authority's multicultural initiatives. Second, 'he had lost the support and trust of many

119

of his parents on account of his insulting and negative statements about ethnic minorities, which were in fact an abuse of his right to free speech' (Halstead, 1988, p. 67). Third, Honeyford had responded to the policies of the local authority externally through the press and other means, rather than internally. Finally, Honeyford had antagonized teachers and parents by his remarks about ethnic minorities and their culture. During the events leading to his early retirement, Honeyford's words were represented and misrepresented in articles, leaflets, speeches and rumour, but Halstead comments:

> Whatever allowances are made for the misunderstanding, misrepresenting or misquoting of what he wrote in his articles, there remains their largely negative tone and a significant core of insulting statements which would be recognised as offensive not only by the committed anti-racists . . . but by many of those 'fundamentally decent people' for whom Honeyford claims to speak. (Halstead, 1988, p. 69)

The reaction against Bradford's policies in Honeyford's writing emerged when the local authority turned its attention towards adjustments in existing educational practices in an attempt to ensure that schools did not discriminate against ethnic minorities. This reorientation of earlier policies followed a period of listening to the ethnic minority communities, understanding the permanence of their presence, and recognizing the validity of their experiences of British culture. In the decade after their publication, the measures in the two memoranda which are concerned with school routines and procedures and racial incidents appear unremarkable and appropriate to the circumstances. Questions can be raised about the refusal of headteachers to consider policies on dealing with racial incidents in the early 1980s. If schools have policies on homework, and if teachers spend time discussing the colour of school uniform, the merits of cardigans rather than jumpers, or the acceptable width of the school tie (provided it is not made of leather), what messages do they convey when they refuse to adopt policies on racial incidents?

The rhetoric of Honeyford's writing is probably an inseparable part of his argument, but there remain some issues which can be considered conceptually and empirically. One of these is the understanding of racism. Honeyford's understanding is that racism is firmly located at the interpersonal level, with no apparent recognition by him of the significance of discrimination by procedures and practices. There is also no recognition of the empirical evidence about discrimination in work or housing available at the time, or of the growing concern about racial harassment and racial attacks. Another limitation is his understanding of the curriculum, its selectivity, its cultural foundations and thus the nature of the school as a cultural institution. Honeyford's concern about academic standards because of the presence of Asian and West Indian children is confounded by evidence on the achievement of pupils in schools (e.g., Tizard *et al.*, 1988; Tomlinson and Smith, 1989).

Honeyford's presumptions about Afro-Caribbean parents' commitment to education are also contradicted by empirical evidence (e.g., Eggleston, 1986; Tizard *et al.*, 1988). In the context of greater understanding of how schools work in a multi-ethnic society which has come through the experiences of teachers and through research, together with awareness of subsequent policy implementation, the grounds of his resistance to change appear insubstantial. However, Honeyford's stance attracted considerable support both locally and nationally. The consequences of the conflict about the issue were deleterious for ethnic and community relations in Bradford, and for the further development of educational policy.

The Dewsbury Schools case – parental choice and white flight?

In Dewsbury in August 1987, parents who had not gained the admission of their children to the school of their choice, having

121

also failed in an appeal to the local authority, and not having succeeded in an appeal for intervention by the Secretary of State for Education, began to prepare for alternative action. A local newspaper, the *Dewsbury Reporter*, recorded:

> parents are prepared to educate their children in a local public house rather than send them to ... the predominantly Asian ... school. They are hoping to enlist the services of volunteer teachers and to use the upper room of the ... Hotel as a schoolroom ... They claim that ... school ... is 95% Asian and their children's education would suffer as a result ...

On 2 September the headteacher of the preferred school found parents and their children who had been officially denied entry at the school door. Newspaper and television reporters were also present. The headteacher talked to the parents and, having found that the children had gained entry to the school, allowed them to stay in the school hall. On the same day some of the parents made applications for a judicial review of the decisions about entry to the schools. That evening there was a meeting between officers of the local authority and the parents which one of the officers later described as 'probably the most hostile meeting of my political career' (Kirklees, 1989).

The demonstrations and attempts to gain entry to the preferred school continued for some time with media attention. The 'school in a pub' continued with help from supporters. A civic occasion in a neighbouring town hall was interrupted. A group called the Parental Alliance for Choice in Education became involved, giving advice and support to the parents. The British National Party sought, unsuccessfully, to be allowed to march through Dewsbury in support of the parents. The parents had begun legal action in November 1987, and changed the grounds of their claim in July 1988. Shortly afterwards the local authority accepted legal advice that the parents should be offered places for their children at the schools of their choice. The offer was accepted by the parents and thus the dispute was brought to an end on 13 July 1988 (Kirklees, 1989).

A prominent element in the interpretation and representation of the parents' action was their rationale for rejecting one school and choosing another. Amongst the complaints referred to in the parents' unsuccessful appeal for intervention to the Secretary of State for Education were reservations about the standard of education in a school with immigrant (*sic*) children, pupils for whom English was a second language. There was also concern about Christian religious education in a school which took account of the religion of its Muslim pupils. Solicitors acting for a group of parents asked the Secretary of State to direct the Council to ensure school compliance with the legal requirements for Christian religious instruction and Christian worship, to 'ensure that the education . . . is efficient, particularly as regards the English way of life, English history and the use of English language'. The Secretary of State was also asked to ensure that the local authority did not discriminate against white children.

These themes of nationality, religion, and skin colour were picked up in the representations of the parents' underlying rationale by the press. As one example, the *Guardian* reported:

> The problem in Dewsbury is, of course, race. Dewsbury shows very clearly that racial fear may be an important stimulus to the exercise of the powers which Mr. Baker is proposing to confer on parents. The parents there may deny any concern about race but cultural anxiety − if that is not too much of a euphemism − is pretty clearly at the heart of the affair. (5 September 1987)

The *Yorkshire Post* expressed sympathy with the parents' point of view:

> They are bound to have misgivings about the educational standards of a school where almost nine from ten pupils are Asian and where many speak as their first language not English but Urdu, Bengali or Gujerati . . . schools with a disproportionate number of Asian pupils are sorely handicapped in their efforts to provide an education which is both equal and English. (4 September 1987)

123

Parental concern about some of the extracurricular features of the school year was reported in the *Daily Telegraph*:

> A spokesman for the parents claims that ... it is a substandard school, that it does not celebrate Christmas and, rather improbably, that chapatis are made there instead of pancakes on Shrove Tuesday. (4 September 1987)

Members of the local authority who listened to the parents were of the opinion that some of the parents made overtly racist comments and that there was an element of racism in some parents' reasoning. One parent allegedly expressed support for 'repatriation' of ethnic minorities. The parents denied that they were thus motivated and their distress at being judged as racist was referred to by counsel during the court hearings. This was not an aspect of the resolution of the dispute and the issue of racial discrimination was left formally unresolved (Kirklees, 1989).

There had been administrative errors in the derivation of admission limits of the schools involved, and it was these which led to the local authority's offer and the parents' withdrawal of action against the authority. Thus the matter of obligations under the Race Relations Act 1976 was not reviewed as part of the case. Section 17 of the Race Relations Act 1976 makes it

> unlawful for an educational establishment to discriminate:
> - in the terms on which it offers admission;
> - in refusing to accept an application;
> - in the way it affords its pupils or students access to any benefits, facilities or services;
> - by refusing to afford them access to these benefits, facilities or services;
> - by excluding them from the establishment or subjecting them to any other detriment. (CRE, 1989c, p. 11)

In addition, segregation on racial grounds would constitute unlawful discrimination.

The Dewsbury case brought the fears of some parents into

prominence, and the manner of its termination aroused concerns that local education authorities might capitulate to parents who were in effect seeking racial discrimination in schools. The dispute did not directly resolve the issues of ethnic and community relations which it exposed. By contrast, it left in its aftermath a number of policy issues for the local education authority, some of them administrative, and others to do with its relations with the community, particularly the ethnic minority communities, whose voices and participation played little part in the dispute (Kirklees, 1989).

The issue of response to parental preferences on grounds which have bearing upon the Race Relations Act has been taken further following the actions of another local education authority. In November 1987 a mother asked her local education authority to transfer her daughter from a school with about 40 per cent Asian children to a school which was predominantly white. A letter written by the mother made reference to the cultural background of the Asian children and to their language. The local education authority allowed the girl to change schools, believing that there was an obligation under the 1980 Education Act to comply with parents' wishes. However, the Commission for Racial Equality ruled that obligations under the 1980 Education Act do not override the requirements of the Race Relations Act of 1976. In its judgment the local education authority broke the law by complying with the parent's request. Following a formal investigation, the Commission for Racial Equality concluded:

> The effect of this is to make it unlawful for a local education authority in carrying out its statutory functions with regard to parental preferences for schools to do any act which constitutes racial discrimination. (CRE, 1989b, p. 11)

In 1990 the Secretary of State for Education challenged the CRE's interpretation of the case, and the CRE sought a judicial review of the issue.

Developing racial equality: the 'race-spies' affair

Local authorities have a duty under Section 71 of the Race Relations Act of 1976 to ensure that their functions are carried out

> with due regard to the need –
> (a) to eliminate unlawful discrimination; and
> (b) to promote equality of opportunity, and good relations, between persons of different racial groups.

One local authority, the London Borough of Brent, which had energetically developed its educational policies within an anti-racist framework from the early 1980s, devised a new programme in the mid-1980s 'to create greater race equality' (Brent, 1987). The programme was designed to utilize funding from the Home Office under Section 11 of the Local Government Act 1966. Section 11 funding can supplement local education authority resources by supporting the appointment of staff, in addition to normal provision, where there may be disadvantages arising from the different languages or customs of ethnic minorities. The programme became public at a time when there had been considerable publicity about the local authority's handling of a situation where a headteacher had made an allegedly racist remark. Reporting on the programme included claims that it was designed to put 'race-spies' in the classroom. In December 1987 the Home Secretary asked Sir David Lane to assess the scheme and its effect upon race relations in Brent. HM Inspectors were also delegated to investigate the scheme.

The London Borough of Brent first adopted a formal policy statement on race equality in 1981 and since then has continued to develop its policies concerned with equality of opportunity with a range of initiatives. The population of Brent includes Irish, Afro-Caribbean and Asian groups, people from other European countries, and a Jewish community. About 40 per cent of the population are black, and about 60 per cent of the children and young people in Brent's schools are black. Sir David Lane reported that race relations in the borough were generally good. They possibly contrast with the experience in rural areas:

> To Brent's credit, race relations in the borough have been relatively relaxed over the years ... Prophets of doom ... have been proved false. This is attributed, among other things, to the tolerance of Brent residents, to the positive attitudes to race relations by all political parties and to sensitive policing ... Yet racism, it is clear from all I have been told, remains a serious menace, not least in the ordeals and problems that children may have to face. 'Paki' shouts can still be heard in playgrounds. Shortly before my inquiry, parties of mainly black children from two Brent schools went on organised visits to Cornwall and the Isle of Wight: they were surprised and shaken to be greeted by racial abuse from some of their rural contemporaries. (Lane, 1988, pp. 7–8)

This much-publicized and much-inspected initiative was entitled the Development Programme for Race Equality (DPRE). Its general aim was 'to enable schools to develop methodologies, structures and curricula which will improve the attainment and life-chances of black pupils and thereby create greater race equality' (Brent, 1987, p. 1). The DPRE was designed to employ teachers who would work in schools with class and subject teachers, supporting their good practice and assisting headteachers, senior management and senior staff. The scope of the work of the DPRE teachers would include curriculum materials and content, classroom methodology, and the school's relations with parents and the community. It would involve support work including analysis of children's language and cultural needs, review of existing resources and practice, monitoring of racist incidents, and the development of new initiatives.

The inspection by HMI (in January 1988) combined school visits, discussions with staff, and observation of home/school liaison activities. While suggesting some modifications to the

127

organization of the programme, HMI's conclusions were positive:

> the evidence suggests that the programme is developing satisfactorily. Most of the work seen in classrooms is of sound quality and addresses the needs of ethnic minority pupils within the normal curriculum . . . The DPRE teachers generally have been welcomed in schools, notwithstanding the publicity surrounding their appointments. (DES, 1988, pp. 23–24)

The HMI report conveys an impression of teachers working co-operatively together in the design and review of curriculum materials, and in the classroom, especially encouraging active oral approaches and the involvement of the community. One account by HMI involved group classroom work on a project concerned with numbers and sorting which entailed the involvement of a parent. Another involved two Egyptian visitors talking about Egypt as part of a project about Africa. The interest, attentiveness and even excitement of the pupils were apparent in the visits. Although HMI noted situations where it was difficult for DPRE teachers to influence the schools, the positive features of the growing partnerships of the teachers were clear in the schools observed. The 'race-spies' allegations were not only false; they were based upon a misconception of the way in which teachers can build positive working relationships. They also underestimated teachers' capacity to work together skilfully in ways which facilitate learning when they are committed to increasing the quality of education.

The Home Office report by Sir David Lane encouraged support for the scheme while suggesting that changes in the management of the scheme be made. The conclusions include an emphatically worded statement, 'Brent deserves praise for a bold and innovative approach to the problem of improving the performance of ethnic minority children in its schools', and a suggestion that it might usefully be adapted by other local education authorities.

Both the Home Office Report and the HMI report comment

on the growth of support from parents, governors and others in the community as the scheme began to take effect.

A playground tragedy and its aftermath

In September 1986 a 13-year-old Bangladeshi pupil was murdered by a white pupil of the same age in the playground of a school in Manchester. The murdered boy had successfully intervened on the previous day to halt the bullying of a younger Bangladeshi pupil. The white boy was reported as shouting a few minutes later, 'I've killed a Paki'.

This tragic event was investigated by a team led by Ian Macdonald, QC. The inquiry's main purpose was to investigate the context of the death, to consider whether there were racial aspects to problems of violence and discipline in the school and other local schools, and to make recommendations about the reduction or elimination of racial harassment, racial violence and racism in schools. Extracts from the inquiry report were first made available in 1987. The report was widely misreported. The full report was published in 1989.

The report examines in considerable detail the background to the murder. It reveals that the white boy had a history of anti-social behaviour and delinquency. It reports on the way in which the school management dealt with the tragedy, the responses of the dead boy's fellow pupils, and the reactions in the community. The analysis of the school includes an account of the management style and the experiences of black teachers in the school. The wider context of the situation was analysed through reference to evidence from other schools in the area and the policies of the local education authority. The misrepresentation of the original report led to the inclusion of a chapter on the way in which the conclusions had been distorted by the media, and the failure of the media to report as widely the team's clarification of the issues.

The inquiry's main conclusions about the murder included the judgements that it was racist but that it raised other com-

129

plex and important issues related to the individual responsible and the culture of violence and male power. The social climate of the school, like that of the surrounding area, included persistent racial violence and abuse. This involved students, but there were also teachers whose actions towards students and members of staff were racist. Although members of the management team had sought to implement an 'anti-racist' policy, they had done so in ways which led to distrust and polarization amongst an already divided staff.

The divisions amongst the staff were clear in the strategies of resistance adopted by some when the issue of racism or equality in the treatment of ethnic minorities was raised. For example:

> A member of staff was grabbed by colleagues and had his face blacked with shoe polish at a party because he was known to support the multi-cultural and anti-racist policies. (p. 140)

> The wearing of pig badges by a large group of staff, many of whom were members of middle management, after the Deputy Head ... had suggested that pork was less suitable than turkey for the school's Christmas dinner, since it prevented Muslim boys from taking part. Pork scratching packets were pinned to his notice board and he was and still is referred to as 'Porky'. (Macdonald *et al.*, 1989, p. 141)

The inquiry team believe that strategies to counter racism are essential for education. However, within the general orientation of anti-racist approaches, they identify, and criticize, a particular model which they label 'symbolic' or 'moral' anti-racism. This model identifies all white people as 'racist', and places the issue of racism 'in some kind of moral vacuum ... totally divorced from the more complex reality of human relations' (Macdonald *et al.*, 1989, p. 402). Thus 'moral' anti-racism divides black from white, emphasizes the guilt of white people and prevents constructive action.

Newspaper reporting of the findings of the inquiry were little related to the content of the report or its conclusions. A number of newspapers attributed the cause of the murder to anti-racism. Others constructed a mythical combination of left-wing fanaticism and anti-racism which were said to have had disastrous consequences. One newspaper generalized from the report, arguing that it raised questions about the policies of numerous local education authorities including Bradford, Berkshire and the ILEA. The inquiry team's recognition of the distortions and misrepresentations was followed by a press statement and conference. They clarified their belief that an effective anti-racist policy would have countered the divisions and violence in the school while distancing themselves from 'moral' anti-racism:

> It is because we consider the task of combating racism to be such a critical part of the function of schooling and education that we condemn symbolic, moral and doctrinaire anti-racism. We urge care, rigour and caution in the formulating and implementing of such policies because we consider the struggle against racism and racial injustice to be an essential element in the struggle for social justice which we see as the ultimate goal of education. (Macdonald *et al.*, p. xxiii)

The reporting of multi-cultural and anti-racist education

Each of the four episodes outlined above was the centre of considerable media attention. That attention included early-morning and late-night calls upon the staff involved. It included the massed presence of radio, press and television journalists in school playgrounds. The quality of reporting (including the presentation of the Brent programme as a scheme to place 'race-spies' in the classroom, and the assertions that 'anti-racism' led to a racist murder) included inaccuracies, distortions and misrepresentations. Some newspapers published fantasies about local authorities banning black plastic bin liners and the banning of 'Baa, Baa, Black Sheep' in playgroups (for example) which later became the substance of folk-myth applied to other places and institutions.

The local authority report on the Dewsbury parents' affair and the Macdonald inquiry report each draw attention to the nature of the reporting and its negative effects. Reviews of the Honeyford case (Halstead, 1988) and the Dewsbury affair (Kirklees, 1989) comment that their impact upon race relations was deleterious (a statement which normally includes an increase in racial abuse and physical attacks upon black people).

This climate of response to policy developments and innovation in education for a multicultural society made progress difficult within some schools and encouraged great caution amongst teachers and headteachers. Nevertheless, many teachers, headteachers, governors and local education authorities persisted with the implementation of their educational strategies.

Conclusions

These four case studies share common features in that they are clustered around the issues of multicultural and anti-racist education. These areas of intersection may not appear large in comparison with the range of concerns which they cover. Those involved were pupils, teachers and headteachers, parents, community organizations, local authorities, central government and the media. The issues of the responsibilities of headteachers versus the local education authority, or parents versus the local education authority, or central government versus local government reveal some of the recent changes in education. The future of developments in education for a multicultural society may rest especially upon some of the recent legislative changes. The prospect of developments under the Education Reform Act and the National Curriculum are considered in the next chapter.

5 Contradictions and new directions

As schools enter the early stages of the effects of the Education Reform Act, grapple with local management, and shape their curricula and procedures to the requirements of a national curriculum and regular testing, there are contradictory visions of the impact of these changes upon education for a multicultural society. There are both pessimists and optimists engaged in social forecasting.

The centralizing effects of the Education Reform Act are regarded with some foreboding by Ball and Troyna (1989). They argue that the Act will lead to the erosion of anti-racist initiatives. They locate the Act in the context of a long-running trend in education which they subtitle 'The Inexorable Rise of the Right'. They predict the end of local anti-racist initiatives:

> Hitherto . . . the structural decentralisation of the education system in England and Wales has permitted a degree of autonomy at the local level. It is within this 'space' that campaigns for racial equality in education have been waged, albeit with different degrees of commitment and vigour . . . The ERA will almost certainly deny this 'space', a prospect which has deleterious implications for the promotion of anti-racism. (Ball and Troyna, 1989, p. 24)

Constraint, or in this case the restriction, of freedom to design new initiatives is but one possible outcome of new structures. Perhaps the new features of the Act will provide new opportunities. These may include new opportunities for the creation of educational divisions through discrimination and a decline in attention to equality of opportunity. Dorn (1990) recognizes this possibility:

> the Education Reform Act brings about changes to the education system that may actually increase the possibility of discrimination occurring. Open admissions, charges for school activities, exemptions from the national curriculum, LMS, standardised methods of assessment and the establishment of new institutions (CTCs, GM schools) create the potential for new forms of discriminatory practices. In addition ERA also involves a major shift in responsibility away from LEAs to governing bodies who are even less likely to be aware of equal opportunity issues rather than LEAs. (Dorn, 1990, pp. 4–5)

There are nevertheless some principles and features which have gained a place in official thinking that were not formally present in the early 1980s. The themes of permeation of the curriculum with multiculturalism and the necessity to ensure that schools deal with issues of racism have informed the work of the National Curriculum Council. A multicultural approach has been identified as one of the dimensions which has implications for the formal and informal curriculum:

> These dimensions have implications for resources, staffing and school organisation, as well as for curriculum content, teaching methods and assessment . . . They require the promotion of positive attitudes in all pupils, and all staff, towards cultural diversity . . . Precise objectives and clear responsibilities for co-ordinating and monitoring work in these dimensions need to be established in each school. (National Curriculum Council, 1989, p. 4)

One of the dangers of 'permeation' is that it may be ineffective as a result of the issues being given so little attention that they are all but invisible. If there are no formal structures of responsibility reaching down into the classroom and out to senior management and the governors, the objectives may be lost. Where these structures are established (or remain in place, since a number of schools already have them) there will continue to be opportunities to renew and adapt multicultural and anti-racist initiatives.

Those with responsibility for the implementation of multicultural or anti-racist policies will be helped by understanding the effects of schools in a multi-ethnic context. Recognition of the importance of particular issues and contradiction of some of the myths about schools and parents have grown out of studies of schools in the middle and late 1980s. The necessary theoretical understanding and the statistical techniques to analyse the data were not available a decade earlier.

Smith and Tomlinson's research into multiracial comprehensive schools (1989) makes it clear that schools can effect a difference. Differences between schools in terms of educational achievement and social ethos have a considerable impact on the careers of their pupils. Moreover, Smith and Tomlinson's concluding sentences confirm the view that multicultural education is concerned with good education: 'The measures that will most help the racial minorities are the same as those that will raise the standards of secondary education generally' (p. 307).

The emphasis put upon education by ethnic minority parents and students is clearly reflected in the findings of studies of schools. Eggleston (1986) emphasized the commitment of young people of ethnic minority origin to their education and their struggle to overcome the obstacles in schools which discriminate against them. This includes their attendance at supplementary schools (Chevannes and Reeves, 1987). Tizard *et al.* (1988) reported that in a study of 33 schools:

> black parents gave their children significantly more help with school work than did the white parents. The black parents were also more positive than the white parents about helping their children in this way ... Black children did significantly more writing at home than white children. (Tizard *et al.*, 1988, p. 94)

In the 1980s there have been changes in many schools designed to remove discrimination against ethnic minority pupils and to provide a curriculum reflecting the multicultural nature of

135

Britain and its place in a global context. These changes have contributed to the moving picture of the comparative educational attainment of ethnic minority pupils. There was justifiable concern about the misplacement of Afro-Caribbean pupils in schools for the educationally subnormal in the 1960s and 1970s (DES, 1985). Another pattern revealed in some studies is of black pupils entering schools with educational and ability profiles similar to those of white pupils but of a gap in educational performance developing in later years (Tizard *et al.*, 1988). Studies of relative patterns of educational attainment have yet to reflect some of the changes in schools in the middle and late 1980s. If these changes are effective there will be higher levels of educational attainment for all groups and new patterns of comparison between the diverse groups in British society.

An optimistic prognosis for the education of a multicultural society in the 1990s would include reference to awareness of the ways in which schools can improve the educational standards of all their pupils and the commitment of many in education to eliminate the reproduction of racism in schools. There were alternative ways of framing an education reform act; for example, by inclusion of explicit reference to cultural diversity and pluralism in education. Nevertheless, the requirement of 'ensuring that all pupils, regardless of sex, ethnic origin and geographical location have access . . .', and similar key phrases tucked into curriculum documents and DES requirements, provides a purchase for further development which was not present a decade earlier. The 1980s was a decade of tussles over the direction of education in a Britain where some were reluctant to admit to the history and permanence of its multi-ethnic and multicultural nature. Perhaps the new generations who emerge from schools and higher education institutions in the future will not only not share that reluctance but contribute to more positive changes towards a pluralist society where schools will benefit all pupils, irrespective of their cultural or ethnic origins.

Bibliography

Aboud, F. (1988), *Children and Prejudice*. Oxford, Blackwell.

Arora, R. K. and Duncan, C. G. (1986), *Multicultural Education: Towards Good Practice*. London, Routledge.

Baker, J. (1987), *Arguing for Equality*. London, Verso.

Baker, J. R. (1974), *Race*. London, Oxford University Press.

Ball, W. and Troyna, B. (1989), 'The dawn of a new ERA? The Education Reform Act, "race" and LEAs', *Educational Management and Administration*, 17, pp. 23–31.

Ballard, R. and Ballard, C. (1977), 'The Sikhs: The development of South Asian settlements in Britain', in Watson, J. (ed.) *Between Two Cultures: Migrants and Minorities in Britain*, pp. 21–56. Oxford, Blackwell.

Banks, J. A. (1986), 'Multicultural education: Development, paradigms and goals', in Banks, J. A. and Lynch, J., *Multicultural Education in Western Societies*. London, Holt, Rinehart and Winston.

Banton, M. (1977), *The Idea of Race*. London, Tavistock.

Banton, M. (1983), *Racial and Ethnic Competition*. Cambridge, Cambridge University Press.

Banton, M. (1987), *Racial Theories*. Cambridge, Cambridge University Press.

Banton, M. (1988), *Racial Consciousness*. London, Longman.

Bhachu, P. (1985), *Twice Migrants: East African Sikh Settlers in Britain*. London, Tavistock.

Bhaskar, R. (1989), *The Possibility of Naturalism*, 2nd edn. London, Harvester-Wheatsheaf.

Blackburn, R. (1988), *The Overthrow of Colonial Slavery 1776–1848*. London, Verso.

Booth, H. (1986), 'Immigration in perspective: Population development in the United Kingdom', in Dummett, A., *Towards a Just Immigration Policy*, pp. 109–36. London, Cobden Trust.

137

Bradford Metropolitan District Council (1983). Agreed Syllabus for Religious Education.

Brent Education Committee (1987), *Development Programme for Race Equality.*

Brown, C. (1984), *Black and White in Britain: The Third PSI Survey.* London, Heinemann.

Bryman, A. (1988), *Quantity and Quality in Social Research.* London, Unwin Hyman.

Castles, S., Booth, H. and Wallace, T. (1984), *Here for Good: Western Europe's New Ethnic Minorities.* London, Pluto Press.

Cavalli-Sforza, L. L. and Feldman, M. W. (1981), *Cultural Transmission and Evolution: A Quantitative Approach.* Princeton, Princeton University Press.

Central Statistical Office (1989), *Social Trends.* London, HMSO.

Chevannes, M. and Reeves, F. (1987), 'The black voluntary school movement: Definition, context and prospects', in Troyna, B., *Racial Inequality in Education.* London, Tavistock.

Commission for Racial Equality (1988), *Learning in Terror: A Survey of Racial Harassment in Schools and Colleges.* London, CRE.

Commission for Racial Equality (1989a), *Annual Report: 1988.* London, CRE.

Commission for Racial Equality (1989b), *Racial Segregation in Education: Report of a Formal Investigation into Cleveland Education Authority.* London, CRE.

Commission for Racial Equality (1989c), *Code of Practice for the Elimination of Racial Discrimination in Education.* London, CRE.

Craft, A. and Bardell, G. (1984), *Curriculum Opportunities in a Multicultural Society.* London, Harper & Row.

Craft, A. and Klein, G. (1986) *Agenda for Multicultural Teaching.* York, Longman.

Cummins, J. (1981), 'The role of primary language development in promoting educational success for language minority students', in *California State Department of Education, Schooling and Language Minority Students: A Theoretical Framework.* Los Angeles, Evaluation, Assessment and Dissemination Center.

Cummins, J. (1984), 'Bilingualism and special education: issues in assessment and pedagogy', *Multilingual Matters*, 6.

Daniel, W. W. (1968), *Racial Discrimination in England.* Harmondsworth, Penguin.

Davey, A. G. (1983), *Learning to Be Prejudiced: Growing up in Multiethnic Britain.* London, Edward Arnold.

138

DeFaveri, I. (1988), 'Ten notes on the recent literature on multiculturalism', *Ethics in Education*, 7, pp. 4–5.

Department of Education and Science (1985), *Education for All: The Report of the Committee of Enquiry into the Education of Children from Ethnic Minority Groups*, Cmnd 9543. London, HMSO. (The Swann Report.)

Department of Education and Science (1988), *Report by HM Inspectors on the Development Programme for Race Equality in the London Borough of Brent*. Stanmore, DES.

Dorn, A. (1990), *Advisory Centre for Education Bulletin*, 33, pp. 4–5.

Dummett, A. (ed.) (1986), *Towards a Just Immigration Policy*. London, Cobden Trust.

Eggleston, J. (1986), *Education for Some*. Stoke, Trentham Books.

Employment Gazette (1988) 'Ethnic origins and the labour market', December, pp. 633–46.

Fryer, P. (1984), *Staying Power*. London, Pluto Press.

Futuyma, D. J. (1986), *Evolutionary Biology* (2nd edition). Sunderland, Mass., Sinauer Associates.

Gardner, M. (1959), *Mathematical Puzzles and Diversions*. Harmondsworth, Penguin.

Gerhardt, P., Howard, S. and Parmar, P. (1985), *The People Trade*. London, International Broadcasting Trust.

Giddens, A. (1989), *Sociology*. Oxford, Polity Press.

Greater London Council (1986), *A History of the Black Presence in London*. London, GLC.

Green, P. A. (1985), 'Multi-ethnic teaching and the pupils' self-concepts', in *Education for All*. London, HMSO.

Grieger, R. M. (1971), 'Pygmalion revisited: A loud call for caution'. *Interchange*, 2, pp. 79–81.

Grinter, R. (1985), 'Bridging the gulf: The need for anti-racist multicultural education. *Multicultural Teaching*, 3, pp. 7–14.

Gurnah, A. (1984), 'The politics of racism awareness training'. *Critical Social Policy*, 11, pp. 6–20.

Hallinan, M. T. and Williams, R. A. (1989), 'Interracial friendship choices in secondary schools'. *American Sociological Review*, 54, pp. 67–78.

Halstead, M. (1988), *Education, Justice and Cultural Diversity: An Examination of the Honeyford Affair, 1984–85*. London, Falmer Press.

Hamers, J. F. and Blanc, M. H. A. (1989), *Bilinguality and Bilingualism*. Cambridge, Cambridge University Press.

Hampshire County Council Education Department (1988), *Education for a Multicultural Society*. Winchester.

139

Harris, M. (1975), *Culture, People, Nature*. New York, Thomas Y. Crowell.

Hemmings, R. (1984), 'Mathematics', in Craft, A. and Bardell, G. (eds), *Curriculum Opportunities in a Multicultural Society*. London, Harper & Row.

Hiro, D. (1973), *Black British, White British*. Harmondsworth, Penguin.

Hollis, M. and Lukes, S. (eds) (1982), *Rationality and Relativism*. Oxford, Blackwell.

Home Office (1989), *The Response to Racial Attacks and Harassment: Guidance for the Statutory Agencies*. Inter-Departmental Racial Attacks Group. London, HMSO.

Honeyford, R. (1982), 'Multiracial myths?' *Times Educational Supplement*, 19 November, pp. 20–1.

Honeyford, R. (1983), 'The multi-ethnic nightmare of intolerance'. *Salisbury Review*, No. 4, Summer, pp. 12–13.

Honeyford, R. (1984), 'Education and race – an alternative view'. *Salisbury Review*, pp. 30–2.

Honeyford, R. (1988), *Integration or Disintegration? Towards a Non-Racist Society*. London, Claridge Press.

Houlton, D. (1986), *Cultural Diversity in the Primary School*. London, Batsford.

Humphry, D. and John, G. (1971), *Because They're Black*. Harmondsworth, Penguin.

Institute of Race Relations (1980), 'Anti-racist not multicultural education'. IRR statement to the Rampton Committee on Education. *Race and Class*, 1, pp. 81–3.

Jenkins, R. (1986), *Racism and Recruitment: Managers, Organisations and Equal Opportunity in the Labour Market*. Cambridge, Cambridge University Press.

Kirklees Metropolitan Council (1989), *A Report by the Chief Executive on the Dewsbury Schools Affair, 1987–1988*.

Kirp, D. (1979), *Doing Good by Doing Little*. Berkeley, University of California Press.

Lane, D. (1988), *Brent's Development Programme for Racial Equality in Schools*. London, Home Office.

Lawrence, D. (1974), *Black Migrants: White Natives*. Cambridge, Cambridge University Press.

Leeds City Council (1987), *Anti-Racist Education—A Policy Statement*.

Lewontin, R. C., Kazmin, L. J. and Rose, S. (1984), *Not in Our Genes: Biology, Ideology and Human Nature*. New York, Pantheon.

Lukes, S. (1974), *Power: A Radical View*. London, Macmillan.

Luthera, M. S. (1988), 'Community, housing and the state – a historical overview.' In Bhat, A., Carr-Hill, R. and Ohri, S. (eds), *Britain's Black Population* (2nd edition). Aldershot, Gower.

Macdonald, I., Bhavnani, R., Khan, L. and John, G. (1989), *Murder in The Playground: The Report of the Macdonald Inquiry into Racism and Racial Violence in Manchester Schools*. London, Longsight Press.

Miles, R. (1989), *Racism*. London, Routledge.

Miles, R. and Solomos, J. (1987), 'Migration and the state in Britain: A historical overview', in Husband, C. (ed.), *'Race' in Britain: Continuity and Change*, 2nd edn. London, Hutchinson.

Milner, D. (1983), *Children and Race: Ten Years On*. London, Ward Lock.

Moore, R. (1975), *Racism and Black Resistance in Britain*. London, Pluto Press.

Mullard, C. (1984), *Anti-Racist Education: The Three O's*. National Association for Multi-Racial Education, London.

National Curriculum Council (1989). *NCC News*, June. York, NCC.

Nei, M. and Roychoudhury, A. K. (1982), 'Genetic relationship and evolution of human races'. *Evolutionary Biology*, 14, pp. 1–59.

Ohri, S. and Faruqi, S. (1988), 'Racism, employment and unemployment', in Bhat, A., Carr-Hill, R. and Ohri, S., *Britain's Black Population* (2nd edition). Aldershot, Gower.

Palmer, F. (ed.) (1986), *Anti-Racism: An Assault on Education and Value*. London, Sherwood Press.

Parekh, B. (1986), 'The concept of multicultural education', in Modgil, S., Verma, G. K., Mallick, K. and Modgil, C., *Multicultural Education: The Interminable Debate*. London, The Falmer Press.

Patterson, S. (1965), *Dark Strangers*. Harmondsworth, Penguin.

Pounce, E. (1985), ' "Together": The forgotten contribution of the black Commonwealth in two world wars'. *Multicultural Teaching*, 3, pp. 9–16.

Pryce, K. (1986), *Endless Pressure*. Bristol, Bristol Classical.

Reeves, F. (1983), *British Racial Discourse: A Study of British Political Discourse about Race and Race-related Matters*. London, Cambridge University Press.

Richardson, R. (1985), 'Each and every school: Responding, reviewing, planning and doing', in *Multicultural Teaching: To Combat Racism in School and Community*, vol. III, no. 2.

Rist, R. C. (1970), 'Student social class and teacher expectations: The self-fulfilling prophecy in ghetto education', *Harvard Educational Review*, 40, pp. 411–50.

Rivlin, H. (1973), 'Introduction'. In Rivlin, H., *et al.* (eds), *Cultural Pluralism in Education*. New York, Appleton-Century-Croft.

141

Robson, M. (1987), *Language, Learning and Race – Developing Communication Skills for a Multicultural Society*. York, Longman for FEU.

Rorty, R. (1982), *Consequences of Pragmatism*. London, Harvester Press.

Rosenthal, R. (1969), 'Interpersonal expectations: Effects of the experimenter's hypothesis', in Rosenthal, R. and Rosnow, R. L. (eds), *Artifact in Behavioral Research*. New York, Academic Press.

Rosenthal, R. (1972), 'Pygmalion revisited, revisited: On a loud and careless call for caution', *Interchange*, 3, pp. 86–90.

Rosenthal, R. and Jacobson, L. (1968), *Pygmalion in the Classroom: Teacher Expectation and Pupil's Intellectual Development*. New York, Holt, Rinehart and Winston.

Rosenthal, R. and Rosnow, R. L. (eds) (1969), *Artifact in Behavioral Research*. London, Academic Press.

Royal County of Berkshire (1983), *Education for Racial Equality: Policy Paper, I, General Policy*.

Sachs, Judyth (1986), 'Putting culture back into multicultural education', *New Community*, 13, pp. 195–9.

Samuel, R. (1973), 'Comers and goers', in Dyos, H. J. and Wolff, M. (eds), *The Victorian City: Images and Realities*, vol. 1. London, Routledge & Kegan Paul.

Scruton, R. (1986), 'The myth of cultural relativism', in Palmer, F. (ed.), *Anti-Racism: An Assault on Education and Value*, pp. 127–35. London, Sherwood Press.

Shaw, A. (1988), *A Pakistani Community in Britain*. Oxford, Blackwell.

Shaw, C. (1988), 'Latest estimates of ethnic minority populations', *Population Trends*, 51, pp. 5–8.

Sivanandan, A. (1985), 'RAT and the degradation of black struggle', *Race and Class*, 26, pp. 1–33.

Sleeter, C. E. and Grant, C. A. (1987), 'An analysis of multicultural education in the United States', *Harvard Educational Review*, 57, pp. 421–44.

Smith, D. J. (1977), *Racial Disadvantage in Britain*. Harmondsworth, Penguin.

Smith, D. J. and Tomlinson, S. (1989), *The School Effect*. London, Policy Studies Institute.

Tizard, B., Blatchford, P., Burke, J., Farquhar, C. and Plewis, I. Young (1988), *Children at School in the Inner City*. London, Lawrence Erlbaum.

Tomlinson, S. (1987), 'Curriculum option choices in multi-ethnic schools', in Troyna, B. (ed.), *Racial Inequality in Education*. London, Tavistock.

Tomlinson, S. and Smith, D. (1989), *The School Effect*. London, Policy Studies Institute.

Troyna, B. (1987), 'Beyond multiculturalism: Towards the enactment of anti-racist education in policy, provision and pedagogy'. *Oxford Review of Education*, 13, pp. 307–20.

Troyna, B. and Williams, J. (1986), *Racism, Education and the State*. London, Croom Helm.

Verma, G. K. (ed.) (1989), *Education for All: A Landmark in Pluralism*. Basingstoke: Falmer.

Visram, R. (1986), *Ayahs, Lascars and Princes*. London, Pluto Press.

Wilson, J. (1986), 'Relativism and teaching', *Journal of Philosophy of Education*, 20, pp. 89–96.

Index